# YouTube Cash Cow Automation Secrets

## Without Visual Presence

Emanuel J. Russo

*To BMZh*

Unlock endless profits:
Visit and Subscribe now
**Cash&Cow Secrets** for more Secrets!
(https://www.youtube.com/@cashcowsecrets)

*This guide is your roadmap to generating a new income on YouTube, even without a visual presence. It's designed to equip you with the knowledge, tools, and strategies you need to embark on a successful journey. By the end of this guide, you'll have the confidence and skills to create and grow your YouTube Cash Cow channel, working toward your financial goals.*
*Let's dive in and explore the world of YouTube income generation together.*

# INTRODUCTION

1.The Rise of Faceless Content Creation

2. What is a Cash Cow Channel?

3. The Power of Automation

4. The Anatomy of a Faceless Video

5. Why Embrace Anonymity?

## Chapter 5: Generating Creative YouTube Video Ideas. Creating Videos with Animation Software - page 127

5.1 The Art of Idea Generation

5.2 Translating Ideas into Scripts

5.3 Dive into Animation: Why It Works

5.4 Best Animation Software for YouTube Creators

5.5 Tips for Creating Engaging Animated Videos

5.6 Collaboration Opportunities

5.7 Call-to-Action (CTA) and Engagement

## Chapter 6: The Vital Importance of SEO and Promotion for Your YouTube Cash Cow Channel to "Dominate YouTube with SEO Optimization" - page 132

6.1 The SEO Paradigm

6.2 The Pillars of YouTube SEO

6.3 Embracing Engagement Metrics

6.4 Channel Optimization

6.5 Beyond YouTube: External Promotion

6.6 Analyze, Adapt, and Improve

# INTRODUCTION

In the vast expanse of the digital universe, YouTube stands out as a vibrant galaxy filled with stars, constellations, and infinite possibilities. Among these shimmering entities, a new star class has emerged: the Faceless YouTube Cash Cow channel. These are channels that capitalize on niche content without ever revealing the creator's identity, often leveraging automation tools for consistency and scale. But why opt for such a format, and how can one embark on this faceless journey successfully? Let's delve in.

1.    The Rise of Faceless Content Creation

- **Digital Anonymity:** In an era where privacy is a luxury, faceless content creation offers a haven for those who wish to separate their online endeavors from personal lives.

- **Universal Appeal:** Without a defined face or identity, content can transcend cultural and regional biases, appealing to a wider audience.

- **Freedom of Expression:** Creators can experiment with diverse content forms without the fear of personal judgment or backlash.

## 2. What is a Cash Cow Channel?

- **Passive Income Stream:** These channels, once set up and optimized, can become consistent revenue generators with minimal ongoing effort.

- **Evergreen Content:** They typically focus on content that remains relevant over time, ensuring continuous viewership.
- **Volume Over Virality:** Instead of chasing viral hits, cash cow channels prioritize a steady stream of content, building a compounding effect over time.

## 3. The Power of Automation

- **Consistency is Key:** Regular uploads, even in the creator's absence, can be guaranteed with automation tools, keeping the audience engaged and the YouTube algorithm satisfied.

- **Efficiency:** Automated processes, from video uploads to audience engagement, free up time for content brainstorming and strategy development.

- **Scalability:** With the bulk of operations on auto-pilot, creators can potentially manage multiple channels, multiplying their revenue streams.

## 4. The Anatomy of a Faceless Video

- **Voiceovers & AI Narration:** A blend of human touch and machine efficiency gives life to scripts without revealing the creator.

- **Stock Footage & Animation:** Visually rich and diverse content can be produced using stock libraries or animation software.

- **Engaging Thumbnails:** Even without a face, clickable thumbnails drive viewership.

## 5. Why Embrace Anonymity?

- **Privacy & Security:** Avoid unwanted attention, both online and offline.

- **Flexibility in Content Creation:** Switch between niches, experiment with styles, or even pivot entirely without audience bias.

- **Longevity:** Even if personal circumstances change or priorities shift, the channel can continue unhindered.

## 6. Consistency and Patience

Building a YouTube cash cow channel without a strong visual presence requires consistency and patience. Keep refining your content, analyzing viewer feedback, and adapting to trends within your niche. With time and dedication, your channel can become a lucrative source of income.

*Embarking on a journey to create a faceless YouTube Cash Cow channel is akin to crafting a novel where characters are vivid, the plot is captivating, but the author remains a mystery. It's about leveraging the vast resources of the digital age while safeguarding one's own narrative. As we delve deeper into subsequent chapters, we will uncover the tools, strategies, and secrets to making this venture not just feasible, but wildly successful. Welcome to the faceless revolution.*

# Chapter 1

## INTRODUCTION TO YOUTUBE AND NON-VISUAL MONETIZATION

### 1.1 Why YouTube Is Important for Generating a Cash Cow

Among the myriad of platforms available, YouTube stands out as a premier space for generating a sustainable revenue stream – or as some might call it, a "cash cow." Below, we delve into the reasons why YouTube is a pivotal platform for this purpose.

**Massive User Base:**

- With over 2 billion logged-in monthly users, YouTube is the second largest search engine globally, right after Google. This means your content has the potential to be seen by a vast audience, offering numerous opportunities to monetize.

**Diverse Monetization Strategies:**

- **Ad Revenue:** Once you're part of the YouTube Partner Program, you can earn money from ads shown in your videos.

- **Channel Memberships:** Your fans can opt to pay a monthly recurring fee to get badges, emojis, and access to exclusive perks.

- **Super Chat & Super Stickers:** This allows your followers to pay money to pin comments on live chat during your livestreams.

- **YouTube Premium Revenue:** You earn a share of the revenue when a YouTube Premium subscriber watches your content.

- **Affiliate Marketing & Sponsorships:** Many creators use their platform to promote products and earn commissions or engage in direct partnerships with brands.

**SEO Advantage:**

- YouTube's strong search capabilities mean that well-optimized videos can rank not only in YouTube search but also in Google search results. This dual SEO power provides a further reach and potential for passive income.

We explored the intricate dance of algorithms and how they influence the visibility of your YouTube channel.

Having delved deep into the algorithm's core, it's time to focus on practical and actionable strategies that can elevate your channel's reach.

The potency of well-crafted keywords and descriptions cannot be overstated.

## Keywords: Your Invisible Allies

In the teeming ocean of content that is YouTube, keywords are the lighthouse guiding viewers to the shore of your content.

They are the silent whisper in the algorithm's ear, emphasizing the relevance and quality of your videos. But how do you harness the latent power of keywords?

## Research

The journey begins with research. Tools like Google Trends, YouTube's own search suggest feature, and other third-party tools can be invaluable.

Identify terms associated with your niche, explore their search volume, and assess the competition.

## Optimization

Every video you upload should be a harmonious blend of creative content and strategic keyword placement.

The title, descriptions, and tags are your canvas – paint them with a blend of short-tail and long-tail keywords that resonate with your audience's search intents.

## Descriptions: A Canvas of Opportunity

A video's description isn't just a summary; it's a narrative that can be woven with threads of SEO gold.

It's an opportunity to provide more context, include additional keywords, and improve the video's visibility.

## Clarity and Conciseness

While it may be tempting to stuff your descriptions with keywords, remember that clarity and conciseness are your allies.

The first couple of lines are crucial; they should encapsulate the essence of the video while being rich with targeted keywords.

## Timestamps and Links

Enhance user experience by including timestamps to key sections of your video, especially for longer content.

Add links to your social media, websites, or affiliate products, transforming the description into a portal of engagement.

## Balancing Act

A caveat as we delve into these waters: SEO is a balancing act. While keywords and descriptions are pivotal, they should not overshadow the quality and creativity of your content.

The viewer's experience is paramount, and each video should be a symphony of information, entertainment, and engagement - finely tuned with the strings of SEO.

Action Steps:

- **Research Keywords**: Use tools and analytics to identify potent keywords within your niche.

- **Optimize Each Video**: Infuse titles, descriptions, and tags with a blend of these keywords.

- **Monitor & Adapt**: Utilize YouTube analytics to monitor performance, and be ready to adapt your strategies.

With every video enriched with optimized keywords and descriptions, you're not just reaching viewers; you're connecting with an audience eager and waiting for the content only you can provide.

## Backlinks: The Silent Endorsements

Imagine backlinks as the invisible threads connecting the vast expanse of the World Wide Web. Every link pointing to your YouTube videos is a vote of confidence, a silent endorsement elevating your content's authority and visibility.

## Crafting Quality Content

The genesis of powerful backlinks is undeniably rooted in the quality of your content. It's an immutable law - exceptional content magnetizes links.

Focus on value, uniqueness, and engagement. Be the content creator whose videos are irresistible to share.

## Leveraging Social Media

Social platforms are the bustling marketplaces of the digital world. Each share, retweet, or repost is a potential backlink, a catalyst amplifying your content's reach. But remember, engagement is key.

Interact, respond, and immerse in the community. Be not just a content creator, but a vibrant entity resonating within the social ecosystem

*Remember, SEO isn't just a strategy; it's a dialogue between your content and the viewers. Make every word count.*

## Evergreen Content:

Unlike platforms where content has a short lifespan, YouTube videos can remain relevant and continue to attract views for years. A well-produced tutorial or evergreen content can generate revenue long after its initial publication.

## The Quintessence of Evergreen Content:

In the dynamic digital landscape, the significance of evergreen content transcends the boundaries of blogs and articles; it's a pivotal element for YouTube channels as well.

This form of content remains relevant, offering persistent value that withstands the test of time, consistently driving traffic and engagement.

## Crafting Compelling Audio-Visual Experiences

When visual presence is minimal, the auditory and informational aspects take the center stage.

Engaging scripts, compelling narratives, and valuable insights become the bedrock of your content.

Each video should weave an experience that's both informative and captivating, ensuring the audience's immersion is not reliant on visual elements.

## Strategic Content Curation

We emphasize the importance of a meticulously curated content library. Each piece, intricately crafted, should serve a dual purpose - addressing the immediate concerns of the audience while remaining a relevant resource over the years.

A blend of tutorials, insights, analyses, and expert interviews can fortify a YouTube channel's content repertoire.

## Leveraging SEO to Amplify Reach

SEO is not confined to the textual domain. A YouTube channel thrives on a robust SEO strategy that encompasses keyword optimization, detailed descriptions, accurate tags, and an engaging thumbnail design.

These elements work in unison to augment the video's visibility, thus elevating the channel's prominence in search results.

## Utilizing Analytics for Content Optimization

We advocate for the unwavering focus on analytics. Analyze viewers' behavior, preferences, and feedback to refine the content strategy.

The fusion of quantitative and qualitative data facilitates informed decision-making, fostering the creation of content that resonates with the audience while adhering to SEO best practices.

## Implementing Accessibility Features

Subtitles, transcripts, and clear audio are indispensable. They enhance the content's accessibility, widening its reach.

This inclusive approach not only caters to a diverse audience but also augments the content's SEO, rendering it a preferred choice for both users and search engines.

## The Power of Collaboration

Collaborative efforts with influencers and thought leaders can elevate the channel's authority.

These partnerships foster an exchange of value, insights, and audiences, driving engagement and enhancing the channel's visibility in search results.

## A Symphony of Strategies

In essence, the path to crafting evergreen content for a YouTube channel devoid of visual elements is a harmonious blend of strategic content creation, meticulous SEO, data-driven optimization, and collaborative efforts.

Each element, distinct yet intertwined, weaves a narrative of enduring relevance, ensuring that the channel not only captivates the audience but also ascends the search rankings with unwavering grace.

## Building Trust & Community:

YouTube offers an intimate way for creators to connect with their audience through video. Over time, this fosters trust, which can then be leveraged for various monetization strategies, from selling merchandise to promoting services.

## Unveiling the Path to Authentic Connections

In the realm of content creation, a YouTube channel is not merely a platform for disseminating videos; it embodies a vibrant community where creators and viewers converge, interact, and thrive.

Building trust and forging a robust community isn't an accidental occurrence but a meticulously orchestrated endeavour. We delve into the intricate art of nurturing an intimate connection between creators and their audience, unveiling strategies that transform a channel into a sanctuary of trust, engagement, and mutual growth.

## The Genesis of Trust

Trust is the cornerstone. It's cultivated over numerous interactions, each echoing the authenticity, transparency, and value that a creator embeds in their content.

The genesis of trust is rooted in consistency – both in the quality of content and the narrative that it unfurls.

Creators must ensure that every piece of content, every message, and every interaction is imbued with integrity and value.

## The Dialogue of Engagement

Engagement isn't a monologue. It's a dialogue, an exchange where creators listen as much as they speak.

Acknowledging comments, responding to feedback, and weaving audience insights into content creation are pivotal.

It's through this reciprocity that a channel transcends its digital boundaries, morphing into a living entity, pulsating with the collective energy of its community.

## Personalization: The Bridge to Intimacy

In the digital age, personalization is the bridge to intimacy. It's the subtle art of tailoring content that resonates, that speaks to the audience on a personal level.

This intimacy is fostered through tailored content, storytelling, and a nuanced understanding of the audience's aspirations, challenges, and journey.

It's about echoing the collective voice of the community in every video, every narrative.

## Community Building Initiatives

Initiatives aimed at community building should be intrinsic to the channel's ethos.
Live sessions, Q&A segments, and community polls not only foster engagement but also unveil insights, unraveling the threads that weave the community together.

These initiatives should not be sporadic but integral, weaving a narrative of inclusivity, participation, and co-creation.

## Nurturing a Shared Identity

A YouTube channel's community is characterized by a shared identity.

It's the collective ethos, values, and narratives that unite creators and viewers. Nurturing this shared identity entails celebrating milestones, acknowledging contributions, and fostering a sense of belonging.

It's about echoing the narrative that every member, every voice, is pivotal to the channel's journey.

## Reflections

Building trust and community for a YouTube channel is an intricate dance of strategies, each echoing the ethos of authenticity, value, and engagement.

It's about transforming a digital platform into an intimate space where creators and viewers converge, not just to consume content but to participate in a shared journey of discovery, growth, and co-creation.

In the ensuing chapters, we will explore, in depth, the tools and tactics that can amplify these efforts, transforming every YouTube channel into a thriving, vibrant community.

## Cross-promotion & Synergy with Other Platforms:

Many YouTubers use the platform in conjunction with other social media channels, blogs, or podcasts. This creates multiple touch-points with audiences, driving more traffic and revenue opportunities.

## Unfolding the Cross-Promotional Landscape

In the intricate web of digital content, a YouTube channel does not exist in isolation.

It's an integral component of a broader ecosystem encompassed by social media, blogs, podcasts, and myriad platforms where audiences converge, interact, and consume content.

Here unravels the art and science of cross-promotion, offering a blueprint to weave synergies that amplify a channel's reach, engagement, and impact through strategic alliances with other platforms.

## The Multichannel Approach

A YouTube channel, enriched by content, becomes infinitely more powerful when integrated into a multichannel approach.

This strategy harnesses the unique strengths, audience demographics, and engagement dynamics of various platforms to create a cohesive and amplified brand narrative.

## Synergizing with Social Media

Social media platforms are not merely channels to share YouTube content; they are arenas to extend the conversation, engage the audience, and foster community.

Tailoring content snippets, highlights, and interactive elements specifically for social media can extend the narrative and invite audiences to experience the depth of content available on the YouTube channel.

## Blogs: The Nexus of Depth and Engagement

Blogs offer an opportunity to delve deeper, providing insights, analyses, and narratives that augment the video content.

By intertwining blogs and videos, creators can offer a multi-dimensional experience, where written content and visuals complement and enrich each other, driving engagement and retention.

## Podcasts: The Auditory Experience

Podcasts open avenues to tap into the auditory senses of the audience, offering content that can be consumed on-the-go.

By intertwining podcasts and YouTube content, creators ensure that the narrative is accessible, diverse, and tailored to the varied consumption preferences of the audience.

## Strategies for Effective Cross-Promotion

1. Content Integration

Integrate and tailor content to resonate with the specific audience and engagement dynamics of each platform, ensuring consistency in the underlying narrative.

2. Collaborative Initiatives

Foster collaborations with influencers, bloggers, and creators across platforms to widen reach, diversity, and engagement.

3. Community Engagement

Engage communities across platforms through interactive content, feedback mechanisms, and participatory initiatives.

## 4. Data-Driven Insights

Harness analytics to glean insights, refine strategies, and tailor content to the evolving preferences and behaviors of the audience across platforms.

## Crafting a Cohesive Narrative

The essence of cross-promotion lies in crafting a cohesive, integrated, and amplified narrative that traverses platforms, echoing the brand's value, authenticity, and engagement.

It's not about mere content dissemination but about weaving an enriched, multi-dimensional narrative experience.

## Reflections

*As we delineate the cross-promotional and synergy landscape, the pivotal insight remains the nuanced integration and tailored strategy for each platform.*

*It's about weaving the YouTube channel into the intricate tapestry of the digital content ecosystem, where each thread - be it social media, blogs, or podcasts - is integral, enriched, and amplified.*

*In the chapters ahead, we delve deeper into the tactical nuances, tools, and technologies that transform this strategic blueprint into a tangible, impactful reality.*

## Low Entry Barriers

Starting a YouTube channel requires minimal investment. With a decent camera, which could even be a smartphone, and basic editing software, anyone can start their journey on YouTube.

## Embarking on a YouTube Journey Without a Visual Presence.

## The Dawn of an Inclusive Digital Era

In an age where visual content seems to reign supreme, the notion of initiating a YouTube channel without a visual presence might appear counterintuitive.

However, as the digital landscape continues to evolve, it unveils opportunities where barriers were once perceived.

In this space of boundless creativity, even without visual elements, one can carve out a niche, captivate audiences, and weave narratives that resonate and engage.

## Minimal Investment, Maximal Impact

The inception of a YouTube channel sans visual presence is not only plausible but requires minimal investment.

With basic editing software, a touch of creativity, and a wealth of ideas, aspiring creators can embark upon a journey where content transcends visual imagery, touching souls and sparking engagement through the power of audio and narrative.

## Your Voice, Your Power

Your voice becomes the brush, the narrative the canvas, and every word paints vivid imagery in the minds of the audience.

It's an intimate sojourn where creators and viewers converge, not through sight, but through the shared experience of stories, insights, and conversations that resonate.

## A Dive into the Basics

## Editing Software: The Creative Companion

Basic editing software is your ally in this journey. User-friendly, accessible, and cost-effective, these tools empower creators to edit, enhance, and refine audio content, ensuring clarity, quality, and engagement.

From adjusting audio levels to integrating effects, the software transforms raw recordings into polished content that captivates and engages.

## Content Creation: The Art of Storytelling

In the absence of visual elements, storytelling ascends to prominence. Every narrative, anecdote, and insight is weaved with meticulous care, ensuring that each piece of content is not merely heard but felt, experienced, and cherished.

## Audience Engagement: The Pulse of the Channel

Engagement is the pulse of every YouTube channel. Even without visual elements, creators foster a vibrant community where feedback is acknowledged, responses are celebrated, and every member feels heard, valued, and integral to the channel's narrative journey.

## Unraveling Opportunities

### Podcast Style Content

Embrace the podcast style, where conversations, interviews, and discussions become the soul of the channel.

It's a space where thoughts are unveiled, ideas are explored, and diverse perspectives converge to create a rich, multifaceted narrative tapestry.

### Tutorial and Guided Sessions

Step into the realm of tutorials and guided sessions, where knowledge, skills, and insights are imparted through the nuanced art of auditory communication. It's not about what's seen but what's heard, understood, and internalized.

### Narrative and Storytelling

Unleash the power of narrative content, where stories transport audiences into worlds woven with words, echoing the depth, emotions, and vivid imagery crafted meticulously through auditory elements.

## A Journey of Auditory Resonance

Starting a YouTube channel without a visual presence is not a limitation but an exploration into the profound intimacy of auditory content.

With minimal investment and basic editing software, every aspiring creator is empowered to embark upon a journey where voices resonate, narratives captivate, and every piece of content is a soulful sojourn into the intricate dance of sounds, words, and emotions.

In this space, we're reminded that the essence of connection transcends sight, delving into the profound spaces where souls converge, narratives resonate, and every voice echoes the profound authenticity of human connection.

## Potential for Virality

While not every video goes viral, the potential for widespread visibility on YouTube is unmatched. A single viral video can drastically change the trajectory of a channel, bringing in numerous subscribers and a significant revenue boost.

**The Allure of Virality**

In the enigmatic universe of YouTube, virality isn't just a buzzword—it's a phenomenon that embodies the quintessence of digital triumph.

A realm where content, creativity, and connectivity converge, YouTube unveils a platform where every video harbors the latent potential to transcend boundaries, touch souls globally, and engrave its narrative in the annals of digital legacy.

**A Catalyst for Transformation**

While the algorithm of virality remains mystic, its impact is tangible and transformative.

Not every video is destined to bask in the ephemeral yet intense limelight of virality, yet the potential for widespread visibility on YouTube is unbridled.

A single viral video is not just a content piece; it's a catalyst that drastically alters the trajectory of a channel.

## Content Resonance

Content is the soul, the primal element where virality is conceived. It's where relatability meets creativity, and narratives echo the collective sentiments, aspirations, and curiosities of the audience.

Every viral video is a narrative tapestry that resonates, engages, and captivates.

## Engagement Dynamics

Engagement is the pulse, the vibrant energy that propels content from the digital echelons to the screens and souls of a global audience.

Likes, comments, shares—they are not mere metrics but the echoes of a narrative's resonance, amplifying its reach and impact.

## Algorithmic Affinity

The YouTube algorithm, enigmatic yet influential, is the silent orchestrator of virality. It's where content, engagement, and visibility converge, propelling videos to the coveted 'Trending' echelons, where visibility and impact are magnified.

# The Ripple Effects of Virality

- Subscriber Surge

A viral video is akin to a magnetic force, drawing viewers into the channel's universe. It's a surge, where every view translates into enhanced visibility, and every share augments the subscriber base, transforming a channel from obscurity to prominence.

- Revenue Revolution

The financial implications are profound. Ad revenues, brand collaborations, and monetization opportunities burgeon. A viral video is not just a content piece but a revenue generator, infusing financial vitality into the channel's ecosystem.

- Brand Ascendance

Beyond metrics and financials, virality is an emblem of brand ascendance. It elevates a channel's stature, transforms its narrative, and engraves its legacy in the digital landscape.

A viral video is the herald of a channel's arrival into the apex of digital prominence.

## The Virality Voyage

In the cosmic realm of YouTube, virality is not an accident but an orchestrated symphony of content, engagement, and algorithmic affinity.

While every video may not bask in the intense yet ephemeral limelight of virality, the potential for transformation is intrinsic and unmatched.

Every content piece harbors the latent potency to transform a channel's narrative, turning obscurity into prominence, silence into echoes, and content into legacy.

In this dynamic voyage, channels are not just platforms but cosmic entities, where every video is a star, destined to engrave its luminescence in the infinite YouTube universe.

## Continuous Improvement & Innovations:

YouTube continuously evolves, offering creators new tools, analytics, and features that can help them better engage their audience and monetize their content. This commitment to growth ensures that creators have the resources they need to succeed.

## A Paradigm of Continuous Improvement and Innovation

In the intricate web of digital content creation, YouTube stands as a colossus, connecting over 2 billion logged-in users monthly, bridging gaps, and offering a plethora of content that caters to a diverse audience.

At the core of this robust system is an unwavering commitment to continuous improvement and innovation, a trait that is intrinsically woven into the fabric of the platform.

With every tick of the clock, YouTube evolves, not just in content diversity but also in the tools, analytics, and features it offers to creators.

It is a relentless journey that ensures creators are not just seen and heard but are also equipped with resources to thrive and succeed.

## Evolution

The inception of YouTube marked the beginning of an era, an age where video content could be created, shared, and consumed with unprecedented ease.

However, like any technology, stagnation equates to obsolescence. YouTube recognized that for it to remain relevant, it must not only adapt but also anticipate the changing tides of digital content consumption and creation.

Hence, the unyielding commitment to continuous improvement and innovation was born.

## The Tools of Trade

Content creation is an art, and like any artist, a creator is only as good as the tools at their disposal. YouTube has consistently rolled out a suite of tools designed to make the process of content creation seamless.

From advanced video editing features to more comprehensive analytics, creators are endowed with resources that transform raw creativity into captivating content.

Each update, each new tool is a step towards making the platform not just a stage for content display but also a workshop where art is honed and perfected.

## Analytics: The Compass of Creation

In the world of digital content creation, data is king. YouTube's enhanced analytics offers creators a compass, directing their content creation process to align with audience preferences, engagement metrics, and monetization potential.

Analytics have transcended beyond mere numbers; they paint a vivid picture of the audience, their likes, dislikes, behaviors, and patterns.

Armed with this intelligence, creators can tailor content that resonates, engages, and cultivates loyalty.

## Monetization: The Reward of Craft

YouTube understands that for creators to fully commit to their craft, there must be financial incentives.

The platform's monetization features have continuously evolved, offering creators various avenues to earn from their content.

From ad revenues, channel memberships, Super Chats to the YouTube Partner Program, creators are presented with a bouquet of opportunities to turn their passion into profit.

## The Horizon of Tomorrow

As we cast our gaze into the future, the trajectory of YouTube's evolution is clear – a journey marked by relentless improvement and innovation.

Artificial intelligence, virtual reality, augmented reality, and other frontier technologies are poised to redefine content creation and consumption.

YouTube stands at the forefront, not just adapting but pioneering this brave new world.

YouTube's unwavering commitment to continuous improvement and innovation is a clarion call to creators. It embodies a promise that their art, craft, and voice will not just find expression but will be amplified, refined, and rewarded.

As the platform evolves, so does the art of content creation, and in this symbiotic dance, the audience is treated to a spectacle of rich, diverse, and engaging content that transcends borders and breaks the confines of imagination.

Every creator is thus, not just a content producer but a vital piece in this intricate tapestry of continuous evolution.

## Global Reach:

Your content isn't limited to one geographic location. With YouTube, you have the potential to reach a global audience, allowing for a wider demographic to view, share, and potentially monetize your content.

## YouTube's International Platform

In a world where digital boundaries are rapidly dissolving, YouTube emerges as a universal stage, a platform where creators can broadcast their content to a global audience without the limitations of geographic confines.

This international reach is not just a feat of technological advancement; it's a testament to YouTube's commitment to making content accessible, shareable, and potentially profitable to a worldwide demographic.

## A Global Audience Awaits

Every video uploaded to YouTube has the inherent potential to transcend international borders, linguistic barriers, and cultural differences.

This is a world where a vlogger from a small town can reach an audience of millions scattered across continents, where a musician can touch hearts and souls beyond their native land.

It's a domain where storytellers, educators, entertainers, and influencers are not confined to local audiences but have the entire world as their stage.

## The Power of Accessibility

YouTube's intuitive interface, seamless streaming capability, and multi-language support ensure that content isn't just globally accessible but is also consumable in a manner that resonates with diverse audiences.
Content creators are equipped with tools to add subtitles, translate descriptions, and customize content to suit the cultural and linguistic nuances of different viewer demographics.

## Sharing Beyond Borders

The global reach of YouTube is further amplified by the platform's easy sharing features.

A video can be uploaded in one corner of the globe and shared instantly worldwide, courtesy of social media integrations and embedded links.

Every share, like, and comment propels the content further across the digital landscape, amplifying its reach and impact.

## Monetizing the Global Footprint

YouTube isn't just about sharing content; it's about transforming creativity into profitability.

With a global audience, creators can tap into diverse revenue streams, adapt content to cater to international markets, and attract multinational advertisers.

The YouTube Partner Program stands as a bridge connecting creators to a world of monetization opportunities that are as limitless as the audience they cater to.

## Navigating the Global Landscape

Yet, with this global access comes the responsibility to navigate complex regulatory, cultural, and ethical terrains.

YouTube equips creators with insights, guidelines, and analytics to tailor content that is not just globally accessible but also globally acceptable.

It's a dance between creativity and compliance, innovation and integrity, reach and responsibility.

*YouTube stands as a portal to the world, where content isn't confined by geography but is empowered to reach, resonate, and impact a global audience. It's a narrative of interconnectedness, a story where every upload echoes across the continents, every view a testament to a world united by digital threads.*

*As creators, the potential is limitless, the audience is global, and the stage is set for content that doesn't just reach eyes but touches hearts, crosses borders, and bridges worlds. In the YouTube universe, the world is indeed a global village, and every creator is a global citizen.*

*YouTube's multifaceted ecosystem presents an unmatched platform for content creators and businesses to generate a sustainable cash cow. The blend of a vast audience base, diverse monetization opportunities, and a platform designed for content longevity makes YouTube a prime choice for those aiming to create long-term revenue streams in the digital world.*

*YouTube's importance in generating a cash cow cannot be overstated. Its monetization options, global reach, flexibility, and long-term income potential make it a vital platform for individuals seeking financial success in the digital age. Whether you're looking to supplement your income or build a full-time career on YouTube, the potential to create a cash cow is within reach for those willing to invest time, effort, and creativity into their channel. In the chapters to come, we'll explore strategies and techniques to help you harness the power of YouTube to achieve your financial goals.*

## 1.2 Why Avoid Visual Presence on Your YouTube Cash Cow Channel?

There are many reasons why you might want to avoid appearing on video on YouTube. You could be shy, concerned about your privacy, or simply prefer an anonymous approach. Fortunately, YouTube offers many opportunities to monetize your channel without ever showing your face.

While YouTube is a powerful platform for content creators, not everyone wants to be in the spotlight or show their face on camera. In this chapter, we'll explore the various reasons why some creators choose to avoid a visual presence on their YouTube Cash Cow channel and how this approach can still lead to substantial success.

### 1.   Privacy Concerns

Privacy is a top concern for many individuals in the digital age. Some creators prefer not to reveal their faces or personal lives on the internet to protect their privacy and maintain a sense of anonymity. This is especially relevant for those who share sensitive or controversial content.

## 2. Shyness and Stage Fright

Not everyone is comfortable in front of a camera. Some creators may experience stage fright or shyness, making it challenging to appear on video. Choosing to avoid visual presence allows them to focus on their content without the pressure of being on screen.

## 3. Language Barriers

YouTube has a global audience, and many creators may not be fluent in the language of their target viewers. Creating content without appearing on camera can be a solution, as it relies more on audio and visuals, making language barriers less of an obstacle.

## 4. Focus on Content Quality

For some, the content itself is the star of the show. By avoiding visual presence, creators can put more effort into crafting high-quality, engaging content without the distraction of their appearance. This approach prioritizes substance over style.

## 5. Creative Freedom

Not showing your face on camera provides creative freedom. Creators can experiment with different formats, animations, or voiceovers, allowing them to explore their unique style and storytelling techniques.

## 6. Broader Appeal

Content that doesn't rely on the creator's physical presence can often have a broader appeal. Viewers can focus on the content's value, rather than the personality of the creator. This can lead to a more diverse and engaged audience.

## 7. Avoiding Stereotypes and Bias

In some cases, creators may choose to avoid visual presence to prevent viewers from making judgments based on their appearance, gender, age, or other personal characteristics. This approach allows the content to speak for itself.

## 8. Scalability

Creating content without a visual presence can be more scalable. It may require less time and effort in terms of makeup, wardrobe, and on-camera preparation, enabling creators to produce more content or focus on other aspects of their channel's growth.

## 9. Versatility

Not being tied to a specific on-screen persona or appearance can be liberating. Creators can cover a wider range of topics and genres without feeling pigeonholed into a particular niche.

*While many successful YouTube channels feature charismatic hosts and engaging personalities, it's essential to recognize that there's no one-size-fits-all approach to content creation.*

*Choosing to avoid visual presence on your YouTube Cash Cow channel can be a strategic decision that aligns with your goals, comfort level, and creative vision.*

## 1.3 "Opportunities without visual presence on YouTube Channel to Generate Income"

Throughout this book, we will examine various strategies and techniques that will allow you to create a successful YouTube channel without having to physically appear in the videos. From producing animated content to using voiceovers, there are many creative options available Not showing your face on a YouTube channel doesn't mean you can't generate a substantial passive income. In this chapter, we will explore the diverse opportunities available to content creators who prefer to remain behind the scenes while still building a lucrative YouTube channel.

## 1. Voice-Overs and Narration

One of the most effective ways to create engaging content without appearing on camera is through voice-overs and narration. You can provide commentary, explain concepts, or tell stories using your voice while showcasing relevant visuals, animations, or images. Many successful channels rely on compelling voice narration to captivate their audiences.

## 2. Animation and Motion Graphics

Animation and motion graphics are powerful tools for conveying information and storytelling. Creating animated videos allows you to present complex concepts or entertain your audience without ever needing to step in front of a camera. Animation can be especially effective for educational, explainer, or storytelling content.

## 3. Screen Recording and Tutorials

Screen recording software enables you to create tutorials, software reviews, and instructional content. You can guide viewers through various tasks, software applications, or online tools while explaining the steps in detail. Your screen becomes the visual focus, making it unnecessary to show your face.

## 4. Compilation and Curated Content

Compilations and curated content can be a valuable resource for your audience. By collecting and presenting interesting or entertaining clips, images, or videos from other sources, you can provide value without having to appear on camera. Always respect copyright and licensing rules when creating such content.

## 5. Whiteboard and Educational Videos

Whiteboard-style videos involve drawing or writing on a virtual whiteboard while explaining concepts or processes. These videos are engaging and educational and can be an excellent choice for teaching complex topics without needing a visual presence.

6. Music and Sound Production

If you have a talent for music or sound production, consider creating audio-focused content. This could include composing original music, soundtracks, or audio guides. Music can set the mood for various types of videos, making it a sought-after skill in the YouTube community.

## 7. Podcasting

Podcasting is another avenue that allows you to generate passive income without the need for a visual presence. You can host discussions, interviews, or storytelling podcasts on a wide range of topics. Podcasts can be monetized through sponsorships, ads, and affiliate marketing.

## 8. Written Content and Transcripts

Even in a video-centric platform like YouTube, written content has its place. You can provide transcripts for your videos, making them more accessible and improving SEO.

Additionally, you can create blog posts or eBooks based on the content of your videos, expanding your reach and income potential.

## 9. Collaborations and Guest Appearances

Collaborating with other creators or inviting guest appearances can add diversity and depth to your channel. You can coordinate with individuals who are comfortable on camera while you focus on the content creation behind the scenes. This collaborative approach can attract a broader audience and increase your passive income opportunities.

*There are numerous opportunities for generating passive income on YouTube without the need for a visual presence.*

*The key is to leverage your strengths, whether that's in narration, animation, music, or other forms of content creation.*

*By providing value to your audience through these various means, you can build a thriving YouTube channel while maintaining your preference for staying out of the limelight. In the following chapters, we will explore strategies for optimizing your chosen approach and maximizing your passive income potential.*

## 1.4 "What to expect from this guide to generate a new income"

This book is designed to guide you through the process of creating, managing, and monetizing a YouTube channel without your visual presence. We will explore advanced strategies, useful tools, and successful case studies. At the end of this journey, you will be armed with knowledge and skills to start your own YouTube Cash Cow channel without showing your face. Ready to begin the journey? Keep reading to discover the secrets of monetization on YouTube without appearing in videos.

Welcome to this comprehensive guide on how to generate a new income, specifically focusing on leveraging YouTube as a powerful platform for your financial success. In this chapter, we'll provide you with an overview of what you can expect from this guide and the journey ahead.

## Defining Your Financial Goals

Before diving into the practical aspects of income generation through YouTube, it's essential to define your financial goals. This guide will help you identify what you want to achieve, whether it's supplementing your current income, creating a full-time career, or building a substantial passive income stream. Knowing your goals will guide your decisions and strategies throughout this journey.

## Understanding the YouTube Landscape

To succeed on YouTube, you need to understand the platform's landscape thoroughly. We'll delve into the essentials, including YouTube's algorithms, content trends, and audience demographics. By grasping how YouTube operates, you can tailor your content and strategies for maximum impact.

## Choosing Your Niche and Approach

Selecting the right niche for your YouTube channel is a critical decision. We'll help you explore various niches, ranging from educational content to entertainment, and guide you in identifying the one that aligns with your interests and expertise. Additionally, we'll discuss approaches to content creation, including those that do not require visual presence, to help you find the perfect fit for your channel.

## Content Creation Techniques

Creating compelling and engaging content is at the core of YouTube success. We'll provide insights and tips on content creation, whether you're focusing on narration, animation, tutorials, or other formats. You'll learn how to plan, script, and produce content that resonates with your target audience.

## Monetization Strategies

Turning your YouTube channel into a source of income requires a deep understanding of monetization strategies. We'll explore diverse monetization options, including ad revenue, affiliate marketing, sponsorships, merchandise, and more. You'll discover how to optimize your revenue streams and develop a sustainable income strategy.

## Building and Engaging Your Audience

Your audience is the foundation of your YouTube success. We'll guide you in building and engaging with your viewers, from effective video promotion to community engagement strategies. By fostering a dedicated and loyal audience, you'll increase your channel's growth and income potential.

## Optimization and Analytics

YouTube is a dynamic platform, and staying informed about your channel's performance is crucial. We'll introduce you to analytics tools and optimization techniques that will help you refine your content, improve your reach, and make data-driven decisions.

## Scaling Your Income

As your channel grows, you'll have opportunities to scale your income. We'll explore advanced strategies, such as diversifying your revenue streams, expanding your online presence, and leveraging collaborations to take your YouTube income to the next level.

## 1.5 Crafting Your YouTube Cash Cow: The Power of Strategy

In the bustling world of YouTube, where billions of hours of video content are consumed every day, creating a successful cash cow channel is no small feat. But what sets apart thriving channels from the rest isn't just luck or charisma; it's a well-thought-out strategic approach. In this article, we'll explore the critical aspects of strategy, focusing on defining your goals, identifying your target audience, researching profitable niche markets, and crafting a content plan that will set you on the path to YouTube success.

## Define Your Goals

To begin your YouTube journey, you must first define your goals. What do you want to achieve with your channel? Are you looking to supplement your income, create a full-time career, or build a substantial passive income stream? Setting clear, realistic goals will serve as your compass, guiding your decisions and actions.

Your goals should be specific, measurable, achievable, relevant, and time-bound (SMART). For example, instead of saying, "I want to make money on YouTube," you might set a goal like, "I aim to earn $1,000 per month from my YouTube channel within one year." This clarity will help you stay motivated and track your progress.

## Identify Your Target Audience

Understanding your target audience is pivotal to YouTube success. Your content should resonate with a specific group of viewers who share common interests, needs, and preferences. Conduct thorough audience research to uncover:

1. <u>Demographics</u>: Who are your potential viewers in terms of age, gender, location, and other relevant factors?

2. <u>Interests</u>: What topics, hobbies, or problems are they passionate about or trying to solve?

3. <u>Behavior</u>: How do they consume content on YouTube? What are their viewing habits and preferences?

By crafting content tailored to your target audience, you'll attract a dedicated and engaged following, a crucial component of a thriving cash cow channel.

**Research Profitable Niche Markets**

In a vast sea of YouTube content, niching down is a strategic move. Identifying a profitable niche that aligns with your interests and expertise can give your channel a competitive edge. Research potential niches by:

1. <u>Keyword Research</u>: Use tools like Google Keyword Planner or YouTube's search suggestions to discover trending topics and keywords related to your interests.

2. <u>Competition Analysis</u>: Explore existing channels in your niche. Identify gaps in their content and opportunities for differentiation.

3. <u>Audience Demand</u>: Check if there's a demand for content in your chosen niche. Are viewers actively searching for information or entertainment in this area?

Remember, your niche should strike a balance between your passion and market demand. A niche with high demand but no personal interest can lead to burnout, while a niche you're passionate about but lacks an audience might struggle to gain traction.

## Content Planning

Content is the lifeblood of your YouTube channel, and planning is the heart that keeps it pumping. A structured content plan ensures consistency and quality. Consider the following elements:

1. <u>Content Calendar</u>: Create a schedule for uploading videos. Consistency helps build an audience.

2. <u>Content Pillars</u>: Identify the core themes or categories your channel will cover. This maintains a cohesive identity.

3. <u>Keyword Strategy</u>: Incorporate relevant keywords in video titles, descriptions, and tags to improve discoverability.

4. Unique Value Proposition: Define what sets your channel apart. What unique perspective or expertise do you offer?

5. Video Ideas: Brainstorm video concepts aligned with your niche and audience interests.

6. Production Plan: Plan your video production, from scripting to editing and promotion.

7. Engagement Strategy: Consider how you'll engage with your audience through comments, social media, and community building.

Remember that creating a YouTube cash cow channel is a long-term endeavor. Consistent, high-quality content is key to attracting viewers, retaining them, and eventually monetizing your channel through various strategies, such as ads, affiliate marketing, and merchandise.

*A strategic approach is the cornerstone of a successful YouTube cash cow channel. By defining your goals, identifying your target audience, researching profitable niche markets, and crafting a well-thought-out content plan, you'll position yourself for long-term growth and financial success on the platform.*

*So, embrace the power of strategy, and let your YouTube journey begin!*

In the chapters ahead, we'll explore various strategies and techniques that allow you to thrive on YouTube without ever showing your face on camera.

Whether you're camera-shy, privacy-conscious, or simply prefer a different approach to content creation, there are countless opportunities to build a successful and profitable channel on YouTube while maintaining your visual anonymity.

# Chapter 2

# Anonymity Advantage: Profit on YouTube without revealing your face!

In the age of influencers and personal branding, showing one's face and personality has become almost synonymous with success on platforms like YouTube.

However, there exists a thriving niche of content creators who maintain their anonymity and yet, amass substantial viewership, engagement, and revenue.

The advantages of anonymity range from personal privacy to flexibility in content creation. Let's dive into how you can profit from YouTube without ever showing your face.

## 1. Why Anonymity?

**Personal Privacy:** Not everyone is comfortable with worldwide fame. Anonymity allows creators to keep their personal and professional lives separate. It ensures safety, reduces chances of unsolicited real-world encounters, and avoids the potential drawbacks of celebrity status.

**Behind the Screen: The Power and Privilege of Anonymity on YouTube**

In a world infatuated with the limelight, where fame and visibility are often perceived as the pinnacle of success, there exists a niche but significant cadre of YouTube content creators who choose the path of anonymity.

These are individuals who, despite possessing the talent, insights, and creativity to captivate global audiences, opt for a discrete separation between their online persona and real-life identity.

Here We explore the unique advantages that anonymity confers to YouTube creators, underscoring the freedom, privacy, and safety intrinsic to this choice.

## The Fortress of Privacy

Anonymity is not a retreat but a fortress, a conscious decision to protect one's privacy amidst the sprawling and often intrusive digital landscape.

In the blossoming era of content creation, not every artist seeks the glaring lights of worldwide fame. For many, the ability to create, express, and impact without the accompanying scrutiny of public attention is not just appealing, but essential.

## Safety in the Shadows

The decision to remain anonymous is often rooted in the unequivocal value of safety.

In a world where online visibility can translate into real-world vulnerabilities, anonymity acts as a shield. It reduces unsolicited encounters, mitigates the risk of intrusion, and ensures that the creator's physical space remains unviolated.

In the shadows, content creators find a sanctuary where their art flourishes, unencumbered by the potential perils of public exposure.

## The Dichotomy of Existence

Anonymity fosters a dichotomy of existence where the personal and professional spheres are distinct, yet harmoniously coexistent.

It allows creators to delve into topics, explore narratives, and express opinions with a candidness that might be restrained under the gaze of public recognition.

This separation ensures that the creator's professional endeavors do not bleed into their personal lives, preserving the sanctity of both domains.

## Avoiding the Celebrity Quagmire

While the allure of celebrity status is undeniable, it comes laden with its set of challenges. The intense scrutiny, the invasion of privacy, and the incessant public attention can be overwhelming.

Anonymity offers an escape from this quagmire. It allows creators to amass a following, influence opinions, and drive trends without the encumbrances of fame. It is freedom in the truest sense - the liberty to create, to influence, and to express without constraints.

*As YouTube continues to burgeon, accommodating a diverse array of content creators, the choice of anonymity underscores the platform's commitment to inclusivity.*

*It reaffirms that on this global stage, there is room for every creator, whether they seek the limelight or choose to weave their magic from behind the curtains.*

*Anonymity is not an impediment but a privilege, a testament that in the realm of content creation, the power of content is not diminished by the visibility of the creator but is accentuated by the freedom, safety, and privacy that anonymity endows.*

**Content Freedom:** Anonymous channels often enjoy greater flexibility. Since they're not tied to a personal brand, these channels can switch content types or themes without risking a disconnect with their viewers.

## The Liberated Canvas: Unleashing Content Freedom in Anonymous YouTube Channels

In the versatile world of YouTube, where creators paint their narratives on a digital canvas, anonymous channels emerge as liberated artists.

Freedom from the constraints of personal branding and public image, these enigmatic creators bask in an unparalleled flexibility, crafting and recrafting their content with a freedom that is both enviable and powerful.

This seeks to unravel the dynamics of content freedom that anonymous channels enjoy and explore the opportunities this liberation ushers.

### Unshackled Creativity

Anonymity on YouTube is akin to an unshackled form of creativity. Without a visual presence, creators are not confined by a set image or identity.

There are no expectations carved in stone, no preconceived notions to adhere to, and no public persona to protect.

Every video becomes a blank slate, an opportunity to venture into unexplored territories, experiment with novel themes, and toy with diverse content types.

**The Fluid Identity**

In the absence of a visual presence, anonymous YouTube channels are not cemented into a rigid identity. This fluidity becomes a superpower.

A channel can morph from a tech review hub to a storytelling oasis, from a gaming sanctuary to an educational resource, all without jarring the audience or inducing a sense of disconnect.

The content, unmarred by a fixed identity, becomes the focal point, and viewers align with the narrative rather than the narrator.

## Adaptive Evolution

As trends ebb and flow and viewers' preferences evolve, anonymous channels are uniquely positioned to adapt, transform, and evolve.

There is no inertia of a personal brand, no resistance rooted in an established identity. Change is not just possible but is seamless and natural.

In this adaptive evolution, viewers are treated to a dynamic content landscape that mirrors the pulsating rhythm of the digital space.

## Risk and Innovation

Without a personal brand hanging in the balance, anonymous creators are emboldened to take risks.

They can delve into controversial topics, explore niche themes, and experiment with unconventional content formats.

This risk tolerance is not reckless but is a crucible of innovation. It is where new content genres are birthed, where unconventional narratives find expression, and where creativity, unbridled and unrestrained, reaches its zenith.

*Anonymous YouTube channels stand as testaments to the liberating power of invisibility.*

*In the absence of a visual presence, content becomes a free entity, unbound by identity, unrestrained by branding, and untethered to a fixed image. Every video is an exploration, every upload a new journey. Viewers are not passengers aboard a predictable voyage but are explorers in a content odyssey that is as dynamic, versatile, and unpredictable as the digital cosmos itself.*

*In this world, content is not just king but is a free spirit, weaving its narrative in a space where the only constant is change.*

**Avoid Controversy:** In an era where personal opinions can ignite internet wars, staying anonymous can help in avoiding unnecessary controversies tied to the creator's personal life.

## Navigating the Turbulent Waters of YouTube: Avoiding Controversy and Protecting Your Online Identity

In the digital age where everyone is a click away from being a global publisher, YouTube has emerged as a powerful platform for sharing ideas, entertainment, and education.

With this empowering tool comes a potential minefield of controversies, where a single opinion can ignite internet wars that not only damage the creator's reputation but also affect their personal life adversely.

### The Internet: A Double-Edged Sword

The internet, for all its advantages, is a double-edged sword. In an era where personal opinions can become public in a split second, a YouTube creator's remarks, views, or content can be dissected and contested by millions worldwide.

These dialogues can sometimes turn into severe controversies tying to the creator's personal life, leading to consequences that go far beyond the virtual space.

## The Anonymity Shield

One effective approach to sidestep this imminent danger is by staying anonymous or using pseudonyms.

While this might seem like an extreme step, it is a pragmatic choice for those who wish to separate their professional and personal lives.

This separation acts as a shield, protecting the creator's identity, safeguarding them from potential backlash, and ensuring that their content remains the focal point, not their persona.

## Content Is King

Creators must remember that content is king. It is the quality, relevance, and value of content that attract and retain viewers.

Avoiding controversial topics, especially those that are deeply polarizing or sensitive, can be a strategic move to maintain harmony on your channel.

Always aim to add value, educate, or entertain, steering clear of subjects that can potentially alienate or offend sections of the audience.

## The Art of Neutrality

Maintaining a balanced and neutral stance on contentious issues is another key aspect. While it's almost impossible not to have personal opinions, expressing them with tact, respect, and consideration for diverse viewpoints can mitigate the risks of igniting online conflicts.

Transparency, respect, and diplomacy should be the guiding principles for any content shared online.

## Social Media Literacy

Equipping oneself with social media literacy is crucial. Understanding the dynamics, trends, and unwritten rules of online interactions can be an asset.
Being informed and prepared is the best defense against the unforeseen challenges that the virtual world often throws up.

*While YouTube offers a potent platform for content creators to reach millions, it is imbued with inherent risks related to privacy and controversy.*

*Staying anonymous, focusing on quality content, maintaining neutrality, and arming oneself with social media literacy are effective strategies to navigate this space safely, ensuring that the focus remains on content, not the controversies.*

## 2. Popular Formats for Anonymity on YouTube

**Animation:** Animated stories, explainer videos, or cartoon series can easily captivate an audience. Platforms like Vyond or Toonly make animation more accessible than ever.

**Voiceover and Stock Footage:** Combine voiceovers with stock footage, images, or animations. Websites like Pexels and Pixabay offer free stock videos and images, while Audacity or Adobe Audition can help with voice recording.

**Tutorials with Screen Recording:** If you're teaching software, design, or any digital tool, screen recordings with voiceovers can be your go-to format.

**Gaming:** Many gaming channels feature just the game's footage and the gamer's commentary without the player's face.

## 3. Crafting Your Anonymous Persona

Just because you're anonymous doesn't mean you shouldn't have a persona. Think of famous anonymous entities like Banksy in the art world. Your voice, content style, logo, and channel name all contribute to your brand identity. Keep them consistent.

## 4. Monetizing Your Content

**Ad Revenue:** Once you cross YouTube's threshold for monetization (1,000 subscribers and 4,000 watch hours), you can earn from ads displayed on your videos.

**Affiliate Marketing:** Integrate product recommendations and share affiliate links in your video descriptions. Every sale generated through your link earns you a commission.

**Sponsored Content:** Companies may approach you for promotions even if you're anonymous. Ensure your content aligns with the product or service being promoted.

**Merchandising:** Create merchandise around your channel's theme or popular catchphrases. Websites like Teespring can integrate with your YouTube channel, making merch selling seamless.

## 5. Maintaining Anonymity

**VPN Services:** Use Virtual Private Networks (VPNs) to hide your IP address when uploading or managing content.

**Separate Email:** Create a separate email ID exclusively for your YouTube channel.

**Stay Consistent:** If you're keen on hiding your identity, avoid sharing personal details, stories, or information that can be traced back to you.

6. Challenges and Solutions

**Engagement:** Without a face, your channel might face challenges with personal connection. Solution? Engage with your audience in the comments, conduct polls, and make content based on their feedback.

**Trust:** Building trust can be a tad bit harder. Solution? Deliver consistent, quality content, and over time, your credibility will be established.

*Anonymity on YouTube is not just a safety measure; it's a strategic choice that can open doors to a world of creativity and flexibility.*

*While faceless, your content can still resonate, engage, and profit. In the end, it's the value and uniqueness you bring to the platform that counts, not necessarily your face.*

# Chapter 3

# Finding Your Ideal Market Niche

In the ever-expanding landscape of YouTube, discovering your ideal market niche is akin to finding the treasure map to your YouTube Cash Cow. This chapter will be your guide to navigating the process of niche selection, helping you unlock the potential for generating income on the platform.

## The Importance of Niche Selection

Before we dive into the "how," let's explore the "why." Why is selecting the right niche so crucial for your YouTube Cash Cow channel? Here are a few compelling reasons:

1. **"Audience Targeting"**: A well-defined niche allows you to target a specific audience with shared interests. These viewers are more likely to engage with your content and become loyal subscribers.

2. **"Competitive Advantage"**: In a crowded YouTube landscape, niching down provides you with a competitive advantage. It helps you stand out and become a recognized authority in your field.

3. **"Content Consistency"**: Niche content is easier to plan and create consistently. This consistency is vital for retaining viewers and building trust.

4. **"Monetization Opportunities"**: Many monetization strategies, such as affiliate marketing and sponsorships, work best within specific niches where you can recommend relevant products or collaborate with industry partners.

5. **"Passion and Expertise"**: Selecting a niche that aligns with your passion and expertise ensures you'll stay motivated and knowledgeable about the topics you cover.

Now that we understand the importance, let's embark on the journey of finding your ideal market niche.

## Step 1: Self-Assessment

Begin by assessing your interests, knowledge, and expertise. What are you passionate about? What do you have substantial knowledge in? Consider your hobbies, professional background, and any unique skills or experiences. This self-awareness will be your foundation for niche exploration.

## Step 2: Audience Research

Next, research your potential audience. Who are they, and what are their interests? Tools like Google Trends, YouTube's search suggestions, and social media platforms can help you identify trending topics and audience preferences. You can also explore online forums, communities, and groups related to your interests to gain insights into what people are discussing and searching for.

## Step 3: Competition Analysis

Examine existing YouTube channels within your areas of interest. Are there established creators covering similar topics? Don't be discouraged by competition; it often indicates a healthy niche. Instead, look for gaps or underserved aspects within those niches. Is there content you can create that isn't currently available or isn't being addressed comprehensively?

## Step 4: Profitability Assessment

Consider the monetization potential of your chosen niche. Are there affiliate programs, products, or services related to your niche that you can promote and earn commissions from? Are there companies willing to sponsor content in your niche? Evaluate the financial viability of your niche in addition to your passion for it.

## Step 5: Niche Validation

Before finalizing your niche, validate it by creating a small amount of content to gauge audience interest and your enthusiasm. You don't need a fully developed channel at this stage; a few videos or blog posts will suffice. Monitor engagement, comments, and viewer feedback to assess the initial response.

## Step 6: Long-Term Commitment

Choose a niche that you're willing to commit to for the long term. Building a YouTube Cash Cow takes time, and consistency is key. Ensure that your niche is something you'll continue to be passionate about and interested in for years to come.

**Potential software and tools for marketer research:**

**- Google Trends**

(https://trends.google.com/): Explore trending topics and research interest over time.

**- YouTube Analytics**

(https://studio.youtube.com): Analyse data and metrics of existing channels in your niche.

**- SocialBlade**

(https://socialblade.com/): Social Blade tracks user statistics for YouTube,

a deeper understanding of user growth and trends.

*Selecting your ideal market niche for your YouTube Cash Cow channel is a critical decision that will impact your success and satisfaction as a creator.*

*By following these steps, conducting thorough research, and aligning your niche with your passion and expertise, you'll be on the path to building a channel that not only generates income but also fulfills your creative ambitions.*

*So, embark on your niche exploration journey with confidence, and let your YouTube Cash Cow thrive in its ideal pasture.*

# Chapter 4

# Researching and Acquiring Quality Content

Running a faceless YouTube channel is an enticing venture for many aspiring creators. The allure of anonymity combined with potential profits has driven a surge in 'Cash Cow' channels. To ensure success, the heart of your channel—content—must be of top-notch quality. This chapter is a deep dive into sourcing and optimizing content for your anonymous YouTube endeavor.

## 1. Understand Your Niche

Before acquiring content, get clarity on your niche.

**Market Research**: Use tools like Google Trends and YouTube Analytics to identify trending topics within your chosen category.

**Competitive Analysis**: Check out top-performing channels in your niche. Note their popular content types and audience engagement strategies.

## Carving Your Space on YouTube: A Deep Dive into Niche Identification and Market Analysis

In the bustling world of YouTube, content creators are presented with both immense opportunities and stiff competition. Amidst the millions of videos that cater to an array of audience segments, a well-defined niche becomes the cornerstone of a successful YouTube channel.

Before diving headfirst into content creation, grasping a concrete understanding of your specific niche is paramount. This clarity serves as the foundation upon which engaging and targeted content is built.

### Step 1: Clarity on Niche

A YouTube niche isn't just a category but a specialized segment of the market you're aiming to engage. It aligns with your passion, expertise, and the unique value you aim to offer to your audience.

Identifying this should be the preliminary step, and it's not to be rushed. Take time to explore and evaluate different niches, considering the audience demand, your personal interest, and the potential for innovation and growth.

## Step 2: Market Research with Technological Aides

In an era where data is king, tools like Google Trends and YouTube Analytics are invaluable for aspiring content creators.

Google Trends helps in identifying the popularity of search terms over time, offering insights into trending topics within a specific niche. Similarly, YouTube Analytics provides a goldmine of data, including viewer demographics, engagement metrics, and content performance indicators.

Leveraging these tools aids creators in aligning their content with current trends and audience preferences.

## Step 3: Competitive Analysis for Informed Strategy

Analyzing top-performing channels in your chosen niche is akin to performing market reconnaissance. It involves scrutinizing popular content types, audience engagement strategies, and the overall content approach of successful creators.

Pay attention to video formats, thematic concerns, and engagement metrics like comments, likes, and shares. This analysis not only offers insights into what works but also helps identify gaps and opportunities to innovate and differentiate your channel.

## Finding the Sweet Spot

The sweet spot emerges where your passion and expertise intersect with audience demand.

It's where your unique value proposition meets an engaged and interested audience. Balancing your interests and strengths with audience preferences and trends, identified through meticulous market research and competitive analysis, is instrumental in carving a distinct and successful niche on YouTube.

## Key Takeaways

Understanding your niche is not a one-off task but an ongoing process of adaptation and evolution. As trends shift and audience preferences morph, continuously engaging in market research and competitive analysis ensures your content remains relevant, engaging, and valuable.

Remember, a well-defined niche is the springboard that can launch your YouTube channel into the realms of success and sustainability, ensuring that your content doesn't just add to the noise but stands out and resonates with a dedicated audience segment.

In conclusion, your niche is the foundation, and understanding it deeply is the first stride in the marathon of YouTube content creation. Armed with insights from market research and competitive analysis, creators are better equipped to tailor content that not only reaches but also resonates with their audience, setting the stage for a thriving and successful YouTube channel.

## 2. Sourcing High-Quality Content

Stock Footage & Images: Platforms like Shutterstock, Pexels, and Pixabay offer royalty-free visuals that can be used for various content formats.
Creative Commons Search: It allows you to find content (videos, music, images) you can legally and freely use. Remember to always give proper attribution if required.
Collaborate: Partner with content creators (writers, voice-over artists) on platforms like Upwork or Fiverr.

# Elevating Your YouTube Channel: A Guide to Sourcing High-Quality Content

Creating a visually engaging and content-rich YouTube channel requires more than just a great idea; it demands high-quality resources to bring those concepts to life. Fortunately, the digital age has facilitated easy access to a wealth of content, from striking visuals to captivating audio.

Let's explore how platforms like Shutterstock, Pexels, and Pixabay, as well as Creative Commons and collaborative partnerships, can be game changers for your YouTube content strategy.

## Stock Footage & Images: A Visual Feast

In the visual-centric realm of YouTube, aesthetics matter. Stock footage and images can enhance the visual appeal of your content without breaking the bank.

Platforms like **Shutterstock**, **Pexels**, and **Pixabay** offer a diverse repository of royalty-free visuals tailored for various content formats. These platforms are user-friendly and provide high-resolution images and videos, ensuring your content is not just engaging but also aesthetically pleasing.

# Creative Commons Search: A World of Free Resources

**Creative Commons Search** is another treasure trove for content creators. This tool allows users to access a myriad of content, including videos, music, and images, which can be used legally and freely.

It's a goldmine for creators looking to enhance their content quality without incurring additional costs.

However, it's pivotal to remember the golden rule of attribution—if required, always credit the original creator in accordance with the specified license.

## Collaboration: The Power of Partnership

While stock footage and Creative Commons are valuable, personalization and customization elevate content to new heights.

Collaborating with content creators can infuse a unique touch to your YouTube channel. Platforms like **Upwork** and **Fiverr** are bustling with talented writers, voice-over artists, animators, and more, ready to collaborate and co-create.
These partnerships not only enhance content quality but also bring diverse perspectives and skills to the table, enriching the overall content experience.

## Balancing Quality and Originality

While leveraging these resources, the importance of originality can't be overstressed. The integration of stock content and collaborations should be strategic, ensuring the channel's unique voice, style, and identity aren't overshadowed.

The goal is to enhance, not replace, original content, ensuring your YouTube channel stands out in the crowded digital space.

*Sourcing high-quality content is an art and science, blending the aesthetic and thematic elements seamlessly.*

*By harnessing the power of stock platforms, Creative Commons, and collaborative partnerships, YouTube creators can elevate their content quality, enhance viewer engagement, and carve a distinct identity in the digital landscape.*

*The key is to strike the right balance, ensuring that each piece of content, while rich and engaging, resonates with the unique ethos and vision of your channel. Armed with these resources, creators are poised to transform their YouTube channels into vibrant, dynamic, and engaging digital spaces where quality content reigns supreme.*

## 3. Voiceovers: The Power of Anonymity

A captivating voiceover can be the linchpin for a faceless channel.

- Hire Voiceover Artists: Sites like Voices.com have a plethora of artists catering to various accents, languages, and styles.

- DIY Approach: If you have a decent voice, invest in a quality microphone and use software like Audacity to record your own.

### The Invisible Magnetism: Unleashing the Power of Voiceovers in Faceless YouTube Channels

In the dynamic sphere of YouTube, where visual content is often king, a growing cohort of successful channels thrives without ever showing a face.

These faceless YouTube channels have debunked the myth that visibility is essential for virality. How, you ask?

The answer lies in the enigmatic allure of voiceovers, a powerful tool that crafts an immersive experience for viewers, drawing them into the world of the content creator without ever revealing their identity.

**The Art of Anonymity:**

There's an undeniable art to maintaining anonymity online, especially in a world that's driven by visual connections.

Anonymity opens the doors to unbridled creativity, offering content creators a space to explore and experiment without the bounds of public scrutiny or personal inhibitions.

The viewer, in turn, is invited into a space of mystery, an enigmatic world where the focus shifts from who is speaking to what is being spoken.

**The Captivating Voiceover:**

A well-executed voiceover becomes the linchpin for faceless channels. It's not merely about delivering content; it's about weaving a sonic tapestry rich with emotions, nuances, and subtleties that captivate the audience.

The voice becomes the identity, fostering a unique connection with viewers that's intimate yet enigmatic.

**Diversity in Voiceover Artistry:**

With platforms like Voices.com, channel owners have access to an eclectic mix of voiceover artists. These platforms are treasure troves of talent, offering a diversity in accents, languages, and styles.

Each artist brings a unique flavor, enabling content creators to tailor the auditory experience of their channel to resonate with a specific audience or to diversify the auditory landscape of their content.

## Crafting an Auditory Identity:

A voice can paint a thousand pictures. For faceless YouTube channels, the voiceover artist's tones, pitches, and cadences become the brushstrokes that create the channel's identity.

It's an art form where the spoken word breathes life into content, transforming ordinary videos into extraordinary auditory journeys that linger in the minds of listeners long after the video has ended.

As the landscape of content creation continues to evolve, the power of anonymity through captivating voiceovers is carving a niche of its own.

In the silent, faceless space, a voice resonates, proving that you don't need to show a face to win hearts, minds, and ears.

In a world overwhelmed with visual stimuli, the enchanting power of a voice stands testament to the adage - sometimes, less is indeed more.

The voice, unbridled by identity, becomes a mysterious force, a narrative element as compelling as the content it unveils, echoing the unspoken yet heard, the unseen yet felt, crafting an experience that's profoundly personal, and yet, universally resonant.

In this silent rebellion against the visual norm, voiceovers for faceless YouTube channels are not just heard but felt, proving that in the enigmatic dance of shadows and echoes, anonymity is not a limitation but a powerful narrative tool of storytelling in the digital age.

## 4. Content Repurposing

Look beyond original content. Repurpose and reimagine existing content to fit your audience.

- Podcasts to Videos: Convert interesting podcast episodes into animated videos or visual slide shows.

- Blog Posts to Explainers: Turn informative blog posts into explainer videos using animations or infographics.

- Books & Public Domain Content: Create summarized versions, reviews, or animated stories.

**Rethinking Content: The Art of Repurposing for YouTube Glory**

In the bustling world of YouTube content creation, the clamor for originality often echoes in the corridors of creativity.

However, an untapped reservoir of potential lies in the art of content repurposing. Refashioning and reimagining existing content isn't a shortcut but a savvy strategy to diversify your content landscape and reach out to a broader audience spectrum.

# The Re-imagination Paradigm:

## 1.    Podcasts to Videos:

YouTube, as a visual platform, offers a unique opportunity to convert auditory experiences into visual masterpieces.

One can transform interesting podcast episodes into animated videos or compelling visual slide shows. It's not just about changing the format but enhancing the content's appeal, making it accessible and engaging for a visual audience.

Every image, animation, and visual element acts as a storytelling device, adding layers of depth and dimension to the auditory narrative.

## 2. Blog Posts to Explainers:

In the age of skimming, explainer videos emerge as powerful tools to convey complex ideas succinctly. Turning informative blog posts into explainer videos is a dynamic form of content repurposing.
By integrating animations or infographics, abstract concepts transform into tangible visuals that not only retain the original message but amplify its impact.

It's a journey from reading between the lines to visualizing beyond the words.

3. Books & Public Domain Content:

The rich tapestry of literature and public domain content is a goldmine for YouTube content creators.

Summarized versions, detailed reviews, or animated stories can breathe new life into classic texts.

It's about transforming the written word into visual narratives, where each frame is a page and every scene a chapter, unfolding stories that have stood the test of time in a format that resonates with the digital audience.

## The Strategic Repurposing

Content repurposing isn't an act of redundancy but a strategic maneuver. It's about understanding the audience, discerning their consumption patterns, and offering content in formats that resonate with their preferences.

Every piece of repurposed content is an original expression, a unique rendition that caters to a specific segment of the diverse YouTube audience.

*In the evolving content creation landscape, the versatility of content is paramount. Repurposing isn't just a creative strategy but an eco-friendly approach in the content ecosystem.*

*It reduces content waste, maximizes resource utility, and amplifies reach. As we step into an era where content is as diverse as the audience it caters to, repurposing emerges as the silent harbinger of an inclusive, adaptive, and dynamic content culture on YouTube.*

*In essence, to repurpose is to reimagine - it's to look at a piece of content not for what it is, but for what it can become.*

*Each podcast, blog post, book, or any piece of content is a seed, and repurposing, the art of nurturing this seed to blossom into diverse gardens of content that cater to the eclectic tastes of the global YouTube audience.*

## 5. Automation Tools

Several tools can assist in automating parts of your content creation process.

- Video Editing Software: Tools like Adobe Premiere Pro or Final Cut Pro have automation features and templates that speed up the editing process.

- Content Scheduling: Use TubeBuddy or Hootsuite to schedule your videos for release, ensuring consistent posting.

**Streamlining Creativity: A Guide to Automation Tools for YouTube Content Creators**

In the digital renaissance age, YouTube stands as a dynamic canvas where content creators paint their narratives. However, the artistry involved is often coupled with the logistical challenges of consistent content creation, editing, and scheduling.

Enter automation tools - the unsung heroes that empower creators to focus on creativity while ensuring efficiency and consistency in content delivery.

**Unleashing Efficiency with Video Editing Software:**

Adobe Premiere Pro

With its intuitive interface and advanced editing features, Adobe Premiere Pro has emerged as a stalwart ally for YouTube content creators.

But beyond its editing prowess lies its automation capabilities. Creators can leverage its rich repository of templates, minimizing the manual effort in crafting visually compelling content. The software's automation features expedite the editing process, transforming raw footage into polished content seamlessly.

Final Cut Pro

For Mac aficionados, Final Cut Pro offers a blend of sophisticated editing tools and automation features.

Its magnetic timeline, coupled with an array of templates, ensures that creators not only sculpt their narratives effectively but do so with speed and efficiency.

Every feature is designed to optimize the editing workflow, ensuring that creativity isn't hampered by time constraints.

# Content Scheduling - The Pulse of Consistency

## TubeBuddy

In the world of YouTube, consistency is as pivotal as creativity. TubeBuddy emerges as a quintessential tool for automating the video scheduling process.

With its intuitive interface, creators can plan their content release, ensuring that the audience is engaged with a steady stream of videos. It's not just a scheduling tool but a strategic asset in audience retention and engagement.

## Hootsuite

Diversifying the spectrum of automation, Hootsuite extends its renowned social media management prowess to YouTube content scheduling.

Its comprehensive dashboard allows creators to schedule video releases, monitor engagement, and analyze performance metrics.

In the seamless dance of content creation and audience engagement, Hootsuite stands as a choreographer ensuring every step, every move is executed with precision.

## Harnessing Automation for Creative Amplification

Automation in YouTube content creation isn't a substitute for creativity but its amplifier. By streamlining editing and scheduling processes, creators are endowed with the luxury of time - time to ideate, create, and innovate.

## The Strategic Intersection

The confluence of creativity and technology is where the modern YouTube content creator resides.

Tools like Adobe Premiere Pro and Final Cut Pro have transitioned from being editing software to creative partners. Similarly, TubeBuddy and Hootsuite are not just scheduling tools but strategic allies ensuring that content not only sees the light of day but does so at the right time, reaching the right audience.

*In the nuanced journey of YouTube content creation, automation tools stand as lighthouses guiding creators through the intricate pathways of editing and scheduling.*

*They ensure that the creator's voice isn't drowned in the logistical challenges but amplified by the strategic, efficient, and consistent delivery of content.*

*In this dynamic landscape, as creators weave their narratives, automation tools are the silent threads knitting the tapestry of creativity with efficiency, innovation with consistency, ensuring that in the ever-expanding universe of YouTube, every story is not just created but heard, seen, and felt by the global audience.*

## 6. Quality Assurance

Never compromise on quality.

- Engaging Thumbnails: Use Canva or Photoshop to design eye-catching thumbnails.

- SEO-Optimized Titles & Descriptions: Use keyword research tools like vidIQ, TubeBuddy or Keyword Tool for YouTube to optimize your video's reach.

- Feedback Loop: Before publishing, get feedback from peers or potential viewers.

## Unleashing Excellence: Quality Assurance Tactics for Your YouTube Channel

In the dynamic and fiercely competitive world of YouTube content creation, the quintessence of a successful channel revolves around two pivotal axes - quality and engagement.

Every aspiring YouTuber should etch the mantra "Never Compromise on Quality" deep into their content creation ethos.

A channel's success isn't merely dictated by the frequency of uploads but is significantly influenced by the quality of each piece of content.

Here We are unveiling a triad of tested strategies to ensure quality assurance for your YouTube channel - captivating thumbnails, SEO-optimized titles and descriptions, and an indispensable feedback loop.

**Engaging Thumbnails**

The first touchpoint of audience engagement on YouTube is undeniably the video thumbnail. An eye-catching thumbnail is like the cover of a book - it should encapsulate the essence of the video's content in an aesthetically pleasing and attention-grabbing manner.

Platforms like **Canva** and **Photoshop** emerge as quintessential tools in the arsenal of a content creator.

Canva's user-friendly interface and plethora of templates offer a quick yet effective means to design engaging thumbnails, while Photoshop caters to more advanced editing needs, offering an expansive suite of tools and options.

## SEO-Optimized Titles & Descriptions

In the realm of YouTube, a compelling thumbnail must be complemented by an SEO-optimized title and description.

This synergy amplifies the video's reach and discoverability. Tools like vidIQ, TubeBuddy, or Keyword Tool for YouTube become indispensable.

These platforms provide insights into trending keywords and optimize content visibility amidst the YouTube algorithm's intricate web.

A well-crafted, SEO-friendly title and description can exponentially increase your content's reach, driving viewer engagement and boosting channel growth.

## Feedback Loop

Quality assurance is an iterative process, refined through constant feedback and improvement. Before hitting the 'publish' button, involving peers or potential viewers in a feedback loop can provide invaluable insights.

These external perspectives can identify overlooked areas for enhancement, offering a multifaceted view of the content's quality, relevance, and engagement quotient.

This pre-publication review process acts as a crucible for content refinement, ensuring that every video is polished and primed for optimal viewer engagement.

*Embodying a relentless commitment to quality and employing meticulous quality assurance strategies is the linchpin for YouTube success.*

*As content creators, weaving the threads of engaging thumbnails, SEO optimization, and a robust feedback loop into the fabric of your content creation process can catalyze your channel's growth, transforming it into a powerhouse of viewer engagement and loyalty.*

*In the vast ocean of YouTube content, let your channel be the lighthouse, distinguished, and revered for its unwavering adherence to quality.*

## 7. Addressing Copyright Issues

Stay vigilant about copyright.

- Avoid Direct Republishing: Always add value through editing, commentary, or transformation.

- YouTube's Audio Library: Utilize YouTube's royalty-free music and sound effects.

- Fair Use Doctrine: Familiarize yourself with the concept of 'Fair Use'. However, remember that it's a legal gray area and can be subjective.

## A Comprehensive Guide for YouTube Content Creators

In the digital age, content creation has blossomed, with platforms like YouTube leading the charge. While this platform offers a space for creativity and expression, it also presents challenges, one of the most notable being copyright issues.

Content creators are often faced with the daunting task of ensuring that their content adheres to legal and ethical standards.

Here, we explore effective strategies for addressing copyright issues and fostering a YouTube channel that's both successful and compliant with legal norms.

## 1. Stay Vigilant About Copyright

In the world of instant content sharing, staying updated on copyright laws is paramount. You should consistently monitor updates in regulations and trends in copyright claims. Join forums, follow legal blogs, and consider seeking advice from a legal professional specialized in digital content.

They can provide personalized advice based on your content type and ensure you steer clear of potential legal hurdles.

## 2. Avoid Direct Republishing: Add Value

Directly republishing content, be it music, video clips, or images, can quickly lead to copyright infringement. Instead, focus on adding value by integrating original elements that transform the content.

This can include insightful commentary, educational annotations, or a creative remix. This not only helps in addressing copyright issues but also enhances audience engagement by offering something new and unique.

## 3. Leverage YouTube's Audio Library

YouTube offers a plethora of royalty-free music and sound effects in its Audio Library, a resource that is invaluable for content creators.
By utilizing these assets, you can significantly reduce the risk of copyright infringement while enhancing the auditory experience for your audience.

Always ensure to follow the usage requirements outlined for each audio file to maintain compliance.

## 4. Fair Use Doctrine: A Double-Edged Sword

The Fair Use Doctrine allows the reproduction of copyrighted material for purposes such as criticism, comment, news reporting, teaching, scholarship, or research.

However, invoking fair use is not a straightforward process. It's often subjective, contingent on factors like the purpose of use, the nature of the copyrighted work, the amount and substantiality of the portion used, and the effect of the use upon the potential market for or value of the copyrighted work.

*Navigating copyright issues on YouTube requires a blend of vigilance, knowledge, and creativity. By staying informed, adding value to repurposed content, utilizing available resources, and treading cautiously around the Fair Use Doctrine, content creators can significantly mitigate the risk of copyright infringement.*

*Always consider seeking legal advice to tailor your approach to your specific content and audience, ensuring that your YouTube channel thrives in a landscape that is both legally compliant and creatively unbounded.*

## 8. Engaging without a Face

A faceless channel doesn't mean an engagement-less channel.

- Engage in Comments: Make it a habit to interact with viewers' comments.

- Polls & Community Posts: Use them to gauge viewer preferences and gather feedback.

**Engaging without a Face: Mastering Audience Interaction on Your Faceless YouTube Channel**

In the dynamic ecosystem of YouTube, the conception that a personal connection stems from putting a face to a name is widespread.

However, in the nuanced space of content creation, faceless YouTube channels are carving out a niche, proving that engagement isn't limited to those who step in front of the camera.

But how do these channels foster a robust, interactive community without ever showing their face? Let's delve into strategies that turn the paradox into a mastered art.

# 1. A Faceless Channel Doesn't Mean an Engagement-Less Channel

The essence of engagement lies in the value and quality of content, rather than the visibility of the content creator's face.

A faceless channel can be as engaging, if not more, by honing in on content that resonates, informs, entertains, and adds value to viewers' lives.

Utilizing voice, animation, screen recordings, or other mediums, faceless content creators can create a unique, memorable identity.

## Building Identity Through Content

The core is consistent, quality content. Visual aesthetics, thematic consistency, and a distinct narrative style can make a channel identifiable and memorable.

It's about weaving a tapestry of content that invites viewers into a world where the creator's identity is ingrained in every video's fabric, though not visible in a physical form.

## 2. Engage in Comments: Make it a Habit to Interact with Viewers' Comments

One of the most direct pathways to engagement is the comments section—a goldmine for fostering a vibrant community. For faceless channels, this becomes an essential tool to compensate for the absence of physical presence.

### Personalized Responses

Every comment is an opportunity. Personalized responses not only address individual viewers but also build a public repertoire of engagement visible to all viewers.

It shows that behind the screen is a creator who listens, values viewers' opinions, and is eager to foster a conversation.

## 3. Polls & Community Posts: Use Them to Gauge Viewer Preferences and Gather Feedback

Faceless doesn't mean voiceless. Polls and community posts are instrumental for channels to vocalize questions, seek opinions, and invite viewer participation.

## Strategic Engagement

Regular polls can be used to gauge viewer preferences, enabling content to be tailored according to audience interests. Community posts can share behind-the-scenes insights, updates, or exclusive content snippets. It's a way to make viewers feel involved in the content creation process, fostering a sense of ownership and community.

## The Art of Faceless Engagement

The landscape of engagement for faceless YouTube channels is not barren but rather a fertile ground where the seeds of strategic, thoughtful interaction can be sown.

By focusing on the quality of content, diving deep into the comments, and effectively utilizing polls and community posts, faceless creators can not only survive but thrive in the competitive world of YouTube.

Ultimately, engagement is an art, sculpted by the consistent, personalized, and strategic interactions that make viewers feel seen, heard, and valued.

In the world of faceless YouTube channels, it's the unseen yet felt presence of the creator that builds a community, one viewer at a time.

*A YouTube automation cash cow channel thrives on the fine balance of quality content, consistent output, and engagement. While maintaining anonymity adds a layer of complexity, it also offers an exhilarating challenge and a unique value proposition.*

*With meticulous research and quality assurance, your faceless venture can stand out and shine amidst the vast universe of YouTube.*

# Chapter 5

# Generating Creative YouTube Video Ideas and Creating Content with Top Animation Software

Anonymity and creativity can go hand in hand on YouTube. The challenge often lies in the generation of fresh, engaging ideas and translating those into visually stunning videos, especially when not revealing your face. This chapter will guide you through the process of brainstorming impactful ideas and turning them into animated masterpieces.

1.  <u>The Art of Idea Generation</u>

*   **Brainstorming Sessions:** Dedicate time regularly to brainstorm topics. Use tools like mind maps or list-making apps like Trello.

- **Stay Updated:** Use platforms like Feedly or Google Alerts to track trending topics in your niche.

- **Audience Engagement:** Tap into your audience's queries and suggestions. The comment section can be a gold mine for content ideas.

- **Competitor Analysis:** Observe top-performing channels in your niche. Aim not to copy but to identify gaps and improve.

## 2. Translating Ideas into Scripts

- **The Power of Storytelling:** Create a narrative around your idea. Even if it's an informational video, a story arc can make it more engaging.

- **Scriptwriting Tools:** Software like Celtx or WriterDuet can help in structuring your scripts.

## 3. Dive into Animation: Why It Works

Animation offers vibrancy, flexibility, and is perfect for anonymous creators.

- **Dynamic Storytelling:** With animation, anything is possible. From flying pigs to talking clouds, your stories can be as imaginative as you want.

- **Universality:** Animated content often transcends cultural and language barriers.

## 4. Best Animation Software for YouTube Creators

- **Adobe Animate:** Ideal for frame-by-frame animations and has a robust set of tools.

- **Toon Boom Harmony:** Used by many professionals, it's perfect for those looking to dive deep into animation.
- **Vyond:** Formerly GoAnimate, Vyond offers drag-and-drop functionalities ideal for beginners or those looking for quick yet quality animations.

- **Blender:** A free, open-source tool not just for animations but also for 3D modeling.

- **Moovly:** A cloud-based software with easy-to-use features suitable for explainer videos.

## 5. Tips for Creating Engaging Animated Videos

- **Keep It Short and Crisp:** Especially if you're just starting, it's advisable to keep videos concise. It maintains viewer attention and reduces production time.

- **Use Voiceovers:** A compelling voiceover can elevate your animation. Consider hiring voice actors or using your voice if you're comfortable.

- **Background Music:** It adds depth to your videos. Use royalty-free music platforms like YouTube's Audio Library or Epidemic Sound.

- **Consistent Branding:** Maintain consistency in animation style, characters, and colors. It helps in brand recall.

## 6. Collaboration Opportunities

- **Team Up with Other Animators:** Share skills, collaborate on projects, or even co-create content.

- **Hire or Outsource:** Platforms like Upwork or Fiverr have numerous freelancers skilled in animation, scriptwriting, or voiceovers.

## 7. Call-to-Action (CTA) and Engagement

- **Engaging without Showing Your Face:** Use animated characters to communicate CTAs like 'subscribe' or 'like'.

- **Polls & Community Posts:** Animation can also be integrated into your community posts or polls, making them more engaging.

*Generating creative ideas while staying anonymous on YouTube is an art, and with tools like animation, you can craft visually rich content that resonates with viewers. Remember, the key lies in understanding your audience, staying updated with trends, and mastering the animation software that aligns with your vision.*

*In the dynamic world of YouTube, it's your unique storytelling and authenticity that will set you apart, face or no face*

# Chapter 6

# The Vital Importance of SEO and Promotion for Your YouTube Cash Cow Channel to "Dominate YouTube with SEO Optimization"

In the vast digital ocean of YouTube, the waves of SEO (Search Engine Optimization) and strategic promotion guide your content to the shores of visibility and virality. Ensuring your channel stands out requires not only quality content but also strategic optimization. This chapter illuminates the paramount importance of SEO and how to leverage it to dominate YouTube.

1.    The SEO Paradigm

- **Algorithm Appreciation:** At its core, YouTube's algorithm aims to provide viewers with the most relevant content. SEO is about ensuring your content is deemed 'relevant'.

- **Beyond Views:** High view counts are great, but YouTube values watch time even more. Optimized videos lead to longer engagement, signaling the platform of your content's value.

## 2. The Pillars of YouTube SEO

- **Keyword Research:** Tools like vidIQ, TubeBuddy, and Keyword Tool provide insights into trending keywords in your niche. Incorporate these into your titles, descriptions, and even scripts.

- **Video Titles:** Concise, engaging, and rich with primary keywords. A title can make or break your video's click-through rate.

- **Descriptions:** Beyond just keywords, craft a description that provides value, perhaps a summary or timestamps. The first two lines are crucial, as they show up in search previews.

- **Tags:** Use relevant tags to provide YouTube with more context. Include a mix of broad and long-tail keywords.

- **Thumbnails:** Though not directly an SEO factor, enticing thumbnails can significantly improve click-through rates, indirectly boosting SEO.

- **Closed Captions:** They make your content accessible to a broader audience and also act as a text source for YouTube's algorithm to understand your content better.

## 3. Embracing Engagement Metrics

- **Comments, Likes, and Shares:** Engage with your audience by responding to comments, encouraging likes, and shares. High engagement signals popularity to YouTube.
- **Playlists:** Grouping related videos can increase watch time. A viewer is more likely to continue watching subsequent videos in a playlist.

## 4. Channel Optimization

- **Channel Description:** A well-optimized channel description gives viewers and YouTube a clear idea of your content niche and value proposition.

- **Featured Video:** Choose a high-performing or a comprehensive introductory video to welcome subscribers and non-subscribers.

- **Consistent Branding:** Use recognizable logos, banner images, and a coherent theme to build authenticity and trust.

## 5. Beyond YouTube: External Promotion

- **Social Media Platforms:** Sharing your videos on platforms like Facebook, Twitter, or LinkedIn increases external traffic.

- **Embeds:** Embed videos on personal websites, blogs, or guest posts.

- **Collaborations:** Partner with creators or bloggers to tap into their audiences.
- **Email Marketing:** For a committed viewer base, consider building an email list to share your latest content.

## 6. Analyze, Adapt, and Improve

- **YouTube Analytics:** Dive deep into metrics like retention rate, traffic sources, and demographic information. These insights help refine future content and optimization strategies.

- **Feedback Loops:** Regularly gather feedback from your audience, peers, or mentors.

*Domination on YouTube isn't about overnight virality but a consistent and strategic push towards visibility and engagement.*

*SEO optimization and promotion are the twin engines propelling your content to its deserving audience. As you hone your SEO skills and synergize them with top-tier content, you not only navigate but also conquer the vast waters of YouTube, establishing your cash cow channel as a beacon for viewers.*

# Chapter 7

# Automation of Publishing and Video Scheduling for a YouTube Cash Cow Channel: The Faceless Efficiency

The hallmark of a truly successful YouTube Cash Cow channel is seamless efficiency. To maintain consistency, drive engagement, and ensure growth without constant manual intervention, automation becomes paramount. Dive into this chapter to explore the intricacies of streamlining your publishing and scheduling processes, all while preserving the anonymity that's crucial to your brand.

1.  <u>Why Automate?</u>

- **Consistency:** Regular uploads keep subscribers engaged and algorithms happy. Automation ensures this consistency.

- **Time Efficiency:** Less manual work means more time for content creation and strategy planning.

- **Optimal Posting Times:** Auto-scheduling tools allow you to post at peak engagement hours irrespective of your time zone or availability.

## 2. YouTube's Built-in Scheduling Tool

- **How it Works:** YouTube's native tool lets you upload a video and choose a future publication date.

- **Private to Public:** Videos remain 'Private' until the scheduled time, after which they automatically switch to 'Public'.

- **Setting Premieres:** This feature allows your subscribers to get a notification ahead of the video's actual release, creating anticipation.

## 3. Advanced Tools for Video Scheduling

- **TubeBuddy:** A certified YouTube partner, it offers advanced scheduling options, best-time-to-post insights, and other growth tools.

- **SocialBee:** While not exclusive to YouTube, this tool helps in promoting your content on other social platforms at optimal times.

## 4. Consistency in Branding with Automation

- **Automated Intros & Outros:** Use video editing software that can automate the addition of intros and outros to maintain a consistent look and feel.

- **Templates:** Develop standardized thumbnail templates that can be automatically applied to new videos, ensuring uniform branding.

## 5. Interlinking Videos for Enhanced Watch Time

- **End Screens & Cards:** Tools like TubeBuddy allow you to bulk add these, guiding viewers to more of your content, thus increasing watch time.

- **Playlists:** Automated tools can be set to add videos to relevant playlists based on keywords or tags.

## 6. Maintaining Viewer Engagement

- **Automated Community Posts:** Engage with your audience using scheduled posts, polls, or teasers about the next video.

- **Response Templates:** While genuine engagement is irreplaceable, having pre-set response templates for common comments can speed up interactions.

## 7. Keeping the Anonymity Veil in Automation

- **Hide Personal Information:** Ensure that none of your automation tools or plugins leak personal information in meta-data or elsewhere.

- **VPN (Virtual Private Network):** Using a VPN during uploads can mask your IP address, adding an extra layer of anonymity.

## 8. Periodic Review and Tweaks

- **Performance Analytics:** Even with automation, regularly review your video performance. Check views, watch time, and engagement metrics.

- **Adjustment:** Algorithms and audience behaviors evolve. Adjust your scheduling times, frequency, or promotional strategies as needed.

## 9. Backup and Redundancy

- **Multiple Backups:** Store content on cloud platforms and external drives. You don't want to lose videos you've prepared for future uploads.

- **Diverse Platforms:** While focusing on YouTube, consider automating content uploads to alternative platforms. This ensures a wider reach and acts as a fallback.

*Automation, when executed thoughtfully, becomes the invisible engine driving a faceless YouTube Cash Cow channel towards success.*

*While it offers undeniable efficiency, the human touch in engagement, content quality, and strategy is irreplaceable.*

*Marrying the two ensures you have a channel that not only thrives in terms of metrics but also resonates authentically with its audience.*

# Chapter 8

# Using Voice-Over and Automated Narration with Best AI Software: The Soundtrack to a Faceless YouTube Empire

For a faceless YouTube channel, voice becomes the powerful bridge connecting content to the audience. With the evolution of AI, automated narration has emerged as a formidable force, offering quality, efficiency, and anonymity. Navigate through this chapter to harness the combined potency of human voice-overs and AI-driven narration for your YouTube Cash Cow channel.

1.    The Power of Voice

- **Building Connection:** Even without a face, a compelling voice can establish rapport, trust, and relatability with your audience.

- **Enhanced Comprehension:** Narration facilitates better understanding, especially for complex subjects or detailed explanations.

## 2. Traditional Voice-Overs:

- **Human Touch:** Natural inflection, emotion, and tone offer authenticity.

- **Customization:** Ability to adjust pace, style, and tone based on content.

- **Cost & Time:** Professional voice-over artists can be costly and require lead time.

- **Anonymity Concerns:** Using your own voice might make some creators uneasy about being recognized.

## 3. AI-Driven Narration: The Future Sound

- **Quick Turnaround:** Generate narrations within minutes.

- **Cost-Effective:** Post initial software investment, it's often cheaper than hiring professionals.

- **Anonymity Guaranteed:** A synthetic voice ensures complete privacy.

- **Lack of Emotional Depth:** Even the best AI may not fully capture the emotional nuances of human voice.

- **Overused Voices:** Popular AI voices might be recognizable across various platforms.

4. Leading AI Voice-Over Software

- **Descript's Overdub:** Create a customized voice using your recordings, which can then produce AI-driven narrations in your style without you continually recording.

- **iSpeech:** Converts text into speech using various voice options and languages.

- **WellSaid Labs:** Offers lifelike digital voices suitable for different types of content.

- **Google Cloud Text-to-Speech:** A product of Google's extensive research in machine learning, offering a wide array of voices.

- **The Best AI Software:** fliki.ai

## 5. Tips for Integrating Voice-Over in Videos

- **Script Precision:** Whether human or AI, ensure your script is clear, concise, and free of jargon.

- **Pacing:** Maintain a steady, understandable pace. While AI voice can be adjusted easily, human narrations might require re-records.

- **Background Music:** Use subtle, non-distracting background music to complement the narration and fill any silent gaps.

## 6. Maintaining Engagement with AI Narration

- **Variety:** Rotate between different AI voices or combine human and AI narrations for different videos.

- **Feedback Loop:** Regularly gather audience feedback on narration quality and adjust accordingly.

## 7. Ethical Considerations

- **Transparency:** If using an AI rendition of your voice or a public figure's voice, consider disclosing this to maintain transparency.

- **Respect Intellectual Property:** Only use voices you have rights to, especially when replicating real voices.

## 8. Evolving with Technology

- **Stay Updated:** AI voice technologies are rapidly evolving. Regularly explore new software or updates to current ones.

- **Hybrid Models:** Consider combining human touch in key content areas (intros, conclusions) with AI narration for main content to achieve efficiency without sacrificing quality.

*Voice, whether emanating from a human or a machine, carries the essence of your content. In a faceless YouTube channel, it's the auditory signature that leaves an indelible mark on the audience.*

*Embrace the fusion of authentic voice-overs and futuristic AI-driven narrations to craft content that not only informs but resonates, all while preserving the sanctity of your anonymity.*

# Chapter 9

# Promotion Strategies and Audience Growth: Becoming the Invisible Magnet of YouTube

Navigating YouTube's vast universe requires more than just stellar content, especially when the creator remains a shadowy figure behind the scenes. It's about magnetizing an audience without being in the spotlight.

This chapter deciphers the intricate dance of promoting a faceless YouTube Cash Cow channel, ensuring its growth and ensuring that the content reaches the right eyes and ears.

1.   <u>The Cornerstone: Understand Your Audience</u>

- **Demographic Profiling:** Analyze which age group, location, and gender resonate most with your content. Tools like YouTube Analytics provide this data.

- **Viewing Habits:** Determine when your audience is most active. This helps in scheduling content effectively.

## 2. Organic Growth: Mastering YouTube's SEO

- **Keyword Research:** Utilize platforms like Google's Keyword Tool or TubeBuddy to find trending keywords related to your content.
- **Optimized Titles and Descriptions:** Ensure your chosen keywords feature prominently here, but remain relevant and non-clickbaity.

- **Engaging Thumbnails:** A picture speaks a thousand words, and an engaging thumbnail can boost organic clicks significantly.

## 3. Playlists: The Serial Engager

- **Themed Playlists:** Group related content into playlists. This encourages binge-watching, boosting channel watch time.

- **Sequential Uploads:** Create series or sequels to hold viewer interest over several videos.

## 4. Collaborate: The Invisible Network

- **Partnerships with Similar Channels:** Even without revealing your face, you can partner with other creators for shout-outs, mentions, or feature your content on their channels.

- **Guest Appearances:** You can do voiceovers or script collaborations with other creators, driving their audience to your channel.

## 5. Leverage Social Media: The Shadow's Echo

- **Content Snippets:** Share short clips or quotes from your content on platforms like Instagram, Twitter, or TikTok as teasers.

- **Engage in Trends:** Participate in trending challenges or topics, driving curiosity-driven traffic back to your YouTube channel.

- **Community Building:** Platforms like Reddit or Quora can be ideal to share knowledge and subtly promote your content in niche communities.

## 6. Paid Promotions: Invisible Doesn't Mean Inaudible

- **YouTube Ads:** Run targeted video ads to promote your content to a broader audience.

- **Influencer Partnerships:** Even without mutual content creation, you can pay recognized figures to promote your channel.

- **Sponsored Posts:** Use platforms like Facebook or Instagram to run posts highlighting your content's USP.

## 7. Engage! Engage! Engage!

- **Heart & Respond:** Regularly heart and reply to comments. It shows activity and encourages more interaction.

- **Polls & Community Posts:** Use YouTube's community tab effectively to engage with your audience, gather feedback, or tease upcoming content.

## 8. Analyze, Adapt, and Iterate

- **Review Metrics:** Regularly check YouTube Analytics to understand what's working and what's not.

- **Feedback Loop:** Encourage viewers to share feedback, adapt your strategy based on constructive critiques.

*Promoting a faceless YouTube Cash Cow channel is an art, blending subtlety with assertiveness. While the creator might remain enigmatic, the content's voice should echo loud and clear across the digital corridors.*

*By weaving together organic growth, strategic collaborations, judicious paid promotions, and relentless engagement, even a faceless entity can carve its niche in the vibrant tapestry of YouTube.*

*Your content, after all, is bigger than any single face – it's a universe in its own right.*

# Chapter 10

# Advanced Monetization Mastery: From Affiliates to Sponsorships on YouTube Automation Channels

Beyond the usual AdSense revenues, there exists a vast landscape of monetization possibilities for YouTube creators. This chapter offers a deep dive into how automation channels, even those without a face, can leverage advanced strategies to significantly boost income and ensure sustainability.

1.    The Monetization Ecosystem of YouTube

- **Beyond AdSense:** Understand that while AdSense provides consistent revenue, diversifying monetization can amplify overall earnings.

- **Tailored Strategy:** Recognize that every channel is unique. What works for one might not be suitable for another. So, personalizing your approach is key.

## 2. Affiliate Marketing: The Silent Seller

- **Choosing the Right Affiliate:** Select products/services that align with your content. Promote products you believe in, enhancing trust and conversion rates.

- **Subtle Integration:** Seamlessly weave affiliate links into your content and description. Avoid being overly promotional, as it might deter viewers.

- **Track & Optimize:** Use analytics to track conversions and click-through rates. Modify strategies based on performance.

## 3. Sponsorships: The Crown Jewel

- **Identify Potential Sponsors:** Look for brands or services that resonate with your channel's niche and audience demographics.

- **Pitching:** Craft a compelling sponsorship proposal highlighting your channel's reach, engagement, and potential benefits for the brand.

- **Integrative Storytelling:** Collaboratively work on content that tells a brand's story without compromising your channel's essence.

## 4. Selling Merchandise & Digital Products

- **Brand Creation:** Even without a face, your channel can have its brand identity. Capitalize on catchphrases, graphics, or any unique element.

- **E-commerce Integration:** Use platforms like Teespring, which directly integrates with YouTube, to promote and sell merchandise.
- **Digital Products:** If aligned with your niche, eBooks, courses, or downloadable assets can be promoted.

## 5. Memberships & Fan Funding

- **YouTube Channel Memberships:** Offer exclusive content, badges, or perks for members who subscribe to your channel for a monthly fee.

- **Patreon & Ko-fi:** Platforms where fans can support creators through donations or subscriptions in exchange for exclusive content or perks.

## 6. Content Syndication & Licensing

- **Repurposing Content:** Your content can be repackaged for other platforms, generating additional revenue streams.

- **Licensing:** If your content is unique and in demand, other platforms or creators might pay to use it.

## 7. Mastering YouTube's Partner Program

- **Maximizing Ad Revenue:** Understand the difference between skippable and non-skippable ads, CPM (Cost Per Thousand) values, and adjust strategies accordingly.

- **Super Chats & Stickers:** Engage with live streaming. Fans can pay money to highlight their messages during live chats.

## 8. Transparency & Ethical Considerations

- **Clear Disclosures:** Always disclose affiliate links, sponsorships, or any paid promotions to maintain trust and adhere to platform guidelines.

- **Avoid Over-monetization:** Striking a balance is crucial. Bombarding viewers with ads or excessive promotions can reduce engagement and trust.

*Monetizing a YouTube automation channel is a blend of strategy, creativity, and ethics. While it's tempting to dive into every revenue stream, it's imperative to align monetization strategies with the channel's essence and the audience's preferences.*

*Remember, trust is the bedrock of any successful YouTube journey. By merging authentic content with well-thought-out monetization, one can truly master the art of YouTube profitability.*

# Chapter 11

# YouTube Channel Management and Success Measurement
## (Mastering the Digital Domain)

The You Tube platform has democratized media production, but with that comes the challenge of effectively managing channels and measuring success in an increasingly crowded space. This chapter delves into the intricacies of channel management and the key metrics by which you can gauge your channel's success.

1.    The Anatomy of a Well-Managed Channel

• **Aesthetics and Consistency:** Your channel should visually represent your brand. From the profile picture to the banner and the thumbnail designs, consistency builds recognition. Ensure that your visuals are high-resolution and reflect the content you produce.

- **Organization with Playlists:** Categorize videos into playlists based on topics or themes. This not only improves user navigation but also increases watch time as videos in a playlist automatically play sequentially.

- **Engage with Your Audience:** Reply to comments, conduct polls, and use community posts to interact. Building a community isn't just about broadcasting; it's about conversing too.

- **Regular Updates and Schedule:** Consistency in uploading can set expectations for your audience. If viewers know when to expect new content, they're more likely to return regularly.

## 2. The Metrics of Success

- **Views and Watch Time:** While views are the most obvious metric, watch time is more indicative of engagement. A video that retains viewers for longer durations is more likely to be promoted by YouTube's algorithm.

- **Subscriber Growth:** Subscribers are your most loyal viewers. A steadily growing subscriber base indicates that your content resonates and appeals to new audiences.

- **Audience Retention:** This graph shows at what point viewers drop off from your video. If many viewers leave in the first few seconds, your intro might need a revamp.

- **Engagement (Likes, Dislikes, Shares, and Comments):** High engagement rates can push your videos into more recommended feeds. Even dislikes can be beneficial, as they indicate interaction.

- **CTR (Click-Through Rate):** This represents how often people click on your video after seeing it in their feed. A high CTR combined with high retention can skyrocket your video's promotion.

3. Understanding and Utilizing Analytics

YouTube's in-built analytics tool provides a treasure trove of data. Regularly reviewing this can give insights into:

- **Demographics:** Knowing the age, gender, and location of your viewers can help tailor content more effectively.

- **Traffic Sources**: Find out how viewers are discovering your content, be it through search, recommended videos, or external sources.

- **Devices**: This indicates whether viewers are watching on mobile, desktop, or other devices, helping you optimize video formatting.

## 4. Adapting to Feedback

Your audience often tells you what they want, either directly through comments or indirectly through engagement metrics. Adapting to this feedback is crucial. If a particular type of content is well-received, consider producing more of it.

## 5. Balancing Monetization and Audience Experience

With YouTube offering various monetization methods, from ads to channel memberships, it's tempting to maximize revenue. However, ensure this doesn't hinder the viewer experience. For instance, too many mid-roll ads can deter viewers from returning.

*Success on YouTube is a blend of art and science. While content is king, understanding the nuances of channel management and the metrics behind your videos is the castle from which the king rules.*

*Embrace analytics, engage with your audience, and always be ready to adapt. In the dynamic realm of YouTube, those who understand their channel's pulse are the ones who truly thrive.*

# Chapter 12

# Understanding YouTube Algorithm Updates

Navigating the Ever-evolving Digital Labyrinth
For any content creator seeking success on YouTube,
deciphering the platform's intricate and frequently updated
algorithm is paramount. But what is this elusive algorithm,
and why does it seem to be in a state of perpetual change?

This chapter delves into the heart of YouTube's decision-
making processes, offering insight into its algorithmic
adjustments and how you can adapt to maximize visibility
and engagement.

1.    A Brief History of the YouTube Algorithm

When YouTube was in its infancy, it prioritized views. The
more views a video garnered, the more visibility it received.
However, this system was flawed, as it unintentionally

promoted clickbait. Recognizing the need for a more refined approach, YouTube shifted its focus to watch time, prioritizing videos that kept viewers on the platform longer.

Over the years, this has been fine-tuned to consider a variety of factors, aiming to provide viewers with content they genuinely enjoy.

## 2. Core Pillars of the Algorithm

- *Relevance*: YouTube uses viewer's search history, liked videos, and other interactions to determine which videos are most relevant to an individual.

- *Engagement*: Videos that prompt interaction (likes, comments, shares) are favored. Such engagement signals indicate a video's value and quality to the viewer.

- *Watch Time and Session Duration*: Not just the duration of a single video view, but the total time a user spends on the platform after watching a video is critical. If your video leads viewers to watch more content, it's deemed valuable.

- *User Satisfaction*: Through surveys and feedback tools, YouTube gauges user satisfaction, ensuring that videos align with what viewers want.

### 3. Why Frequent Updates?

With billions of views daily and ever-evolving user behavior, YouTube's priority is to ensure a positive and engaging user experience. Algorithm updates aim to:

- Address loopholes that may be exploited.

- Adapt to changing viewer behavior and preferences.

- Introduce new features or tools to enhance the platform.

### 4. Adapting to Algorithm Changes

While no one outside YouTube's core team can predict the exact nature of future updates, a few general strategies can keep your channel in good stead:

- **Quality Over Quantity**: Instead of chasing trends or producing mass content, focus on creating valuable, high-quality videos that offer something unique to viewers.

- **Engage with Your Community**: Foster a sense of community among your subscribers. Reply to comments, conduct polls, and listen to feedback.

- **Stay Updated**: Join YouTube's official creator forums, subscribe to the YouTube Creators channel, and network with other content creators. Knowledge is power.

- **Diversify Traffic Sources**: While the YouTube search function is essential, also utilize other platforms and methods to drive traffic to your videos, such as social media and collaborations.

5. Debunking Myths about the Algorithm

There's a myriad of myths surrounding YouTube's algorithm. Common misconceptions include the belief that posting daily is a must or that the platform suppresses certain types of content.

While trends can be observed, it's essential to differentiate between correlation and causation. Always refer to YouTube's official resources or trusted industry experts when in doubt.

*The YouTube algorithm, while complex, has a singular aim: to provide viewers with content they'll love. As creators, our mission aligns with this goal.*

*By understanding the motivations behind algorithm updates and continually striving to produce content that resonates, we can navigate the changing waters of YouTube and reach our desired audiences effectively.*

*Remember, in the dance between creators and the algorithm, adaptability and authenticity are the steps to success.*

# BONUS

# The best AI software for you tube creator

- **TubeBuddy** (https://www.tubebuddy.com/): An all-in-one browser extension and mobile app that integrates directly with YouTube to help you run your channel with ease. It offers a range of tools including keyword research, thumbnail testing, and competitive analysis.

- **VidIQ** (https://vidiq.com/): Similar to TubeBuddy, VidIQ offers a suite of tools to help creators grow their channel. This includes keyword suggestions, SEO tools, and analytics.

- **Magisto** (https://filmora.wondershare.net/): An online video editor powered by AI. It allows users to create videos quickly by selecting a style, adding their content, and choosing music.

- **D-ID** (studio.d-id.com/): Create a video with AI Face.

- **Lumen5** (https://lumen5.com/): This is a video creation platform driven by AI. It's especially useful for turning articles or blog posts into engaging video content.

- **Descript** (https://www.descript.com/): A tool for editing audio and video by editing the text transcript. It uses AI for automatic transcription and offers features like "Overdub" which allows you to create a synthetic voice clone to fix or change parts of your video without re-recording.

- **Clipchamp** (https://clipchamp.com/): While primarily a video editor, it also features AI-driven capabilities, such as optimizing video quality and automating editing processes.

- **Runway ML** (https://runwayml.com/): Offers tools for creators to use machine learning models for video, enabling effects and manipulations that would be difficult or impossible otherwise.

- **Pixabay** (https://pixabay.com/): Stunning royalty-free images & royalty-free stock

- **Lexica** (https://lexica.art/): Is an AI art platform that allows users to generate images using user prompts.

- **Aiva** (https://www.aiva.ai/): An AI music composer. This is great for YouTube creators in need of unique background music for their content without copyright issues.

- **Pex** (https://pex.com/): It's an AI-powered tool that allows creators to find where and how their content is being used across the internet. This is especially useful to track unauthorized copies or usage of one's content.

- **Remini** (https://remini.ai/): An AI photo enhancer app which can also be used to enhance the quality of video footage, especially useful for upscaling old or low-resolution videos.

- **ChatGPT** (https://chat.openai.com/): A virtual conversational assistant powered by OpenAI's language model.

It's important to note that the world of AI is rapidly evolving.

New tools and software are regularly being developed, and the effectiveness of any platform can vary based on individual needs and content types.

Always look for reviews and perhaps test out a few different options before committing to a specific tool, so **for more AI Software for You Tube Creators visit:**

**Futurepedia.io**
(https://www.futurepedia.io/):

Is the go-place for AI tools and news. Futurepedia also provides insights into the future of AI content, about post, image, and video.

* Thanks to Guillaume Meurice for the imagine of cover
  (pexels.com)